W9-BMM-904

SHARK
QUEST

PROTECTING THE OCEAN'S TOP PREDATORS

KAREN ROMANO YOUNG

TWENTY-FIRST CENTURY BOOKS / MINNEAPOLIS

FOR ELLIOTT AND LIAM

Text copyright © 2019 by Karen Romano Young

All rights reserved. International copyright secured. No part of this book may be reproduced, stored in a retrieval system, or transmitted in any form or by any means—electronic, mechanical, photocopying, recording, or otherwise—without the prior written permission of Lerner Publishing Group, Inc., except for the inclusion of brief quotations in an acknowledged review.

Twenty-First Century Books
A division of Lerner Publishing Group, Inc.
241 First Avenue North
Minneapolis, MN 55401 USA

For reading levels and more information, look up this title at www.lernerbooks.com.

Main body text set in Adobe Garamond Pro 11/15.
Typeface provided by Adobe Systems.

Library of Congress Cataloging-in-Publication Data

Names: Young, Karen Romano, author.
Title: Shark quest : protecting the ocean's top predators / Karen Romano Young.
Description: Minneapolis : Twenty-First Century Books, [2018] | Audience: Ages 13–18. | Audience: Grades 9 to 12. | Includes bibliographical references and index.
Identifiers: LCCN 2017044282 (print) | LCCN 2017048881 (ebook) | ISBN 9781541524811 (eb pdf) | ISBN 9781512498059 (lb : alk. paper)
Subjects: LCSH: Sharks—Conservation—Juvenile literature. | Sharks—Behavior—Juvenile literature.
Classification: LCC QL638.9 (ebook) | LCC QL638.9 .Y55 2018 (print) | DDC 597.3—dc23

LC record available at https://lccn.loc.gov/2017044282

Manufactured in the United States of America
1-43545-33330-2/9/2018

CONTENTS

1

THE **TROUBLE** WITH **SHARKS**   4

2

WHAT'S A **SHARK**?   18

3

FEEDING THE **BEAST**   32

4

SHARK **SEX**   44

5

SWIMMING WITH **SHARKS**   52

6

WHAT DO **SHARK**
RESEARCHERS DO AT **SEA**?   66

7

WHAT DO **SHARK**
RESEARCHERS DO **ONSHORE**?   80

8

CITIZEN SCIENCE FOR
THE **SHARKS**   90

SHARK GUIDE   106

SOURCE NOTES   115

GLOSSARY   118

SELECTED BIBLIOGRAPHY   120

FURTHER INFORMATION   121

INDEX   125

1

THE **TROUBLE** WITH **SHARKS**

THE RELEASE OF [THE 1975 MOVIE] *JAWS* CONTRIBUTED TO PEOPLE WANTING TO EXTERMINATE SHARKS. SHARKS HAVE MUCH MORE CAUSE TO FEAR HUMANS. TODAY SHARKS ARE DECREASING IN ALL OCEANS BECAUSE OF HUMAN ACTIVITY.

—ALESSANDRO DE MADDALENA,
SHARK EXPERT, IN *SHARKS OF NEW ENGLAND*, 2010

Peter Benchley was a lifelong swimmer and diver, well known as the author of the best-selling book *Jaws*, published in 1974. The novel was inspired by a newspaper story describing a massive 4,550-pound (2,064 kg) great white shark caught off Long Island, New York. Set in a beach community, *Jaws* features fictional characters: a gigantic, vicious shark; a marine biologist; and a local sheriff seeking to stop the shark's human-killing spree. When the movie adaptation of *Jaws* was released the next year, it unleashed nightmares from the dungeons of the human mind all over the world. "People are, and always have

The 1975 film *Jaws* is one of the most famous American thrillers of all time. Directed by Steven Spielberg, it won three Academy Awards. In 2001 the film was selected for preservation in the United States National Film Registry. All the same, many critics say the movie has created negative and unrealistic stereotypes of shark behavior that persist into the twenty-first century.

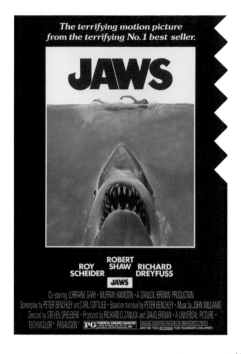

bcen, both intrigued and terrified by sharks," said Benchley, who died in 2006. "Sharks come from one part of the dark castle where our nightmares live—the deep water beyond our sight and understanding. So they stimulate our fears and our fantasies."

Two hundred years earlier, in 1778, the *East London Advertiser* featured the eyewitness account of a vicious tiger shark attack on Brook Watson, a fourteen-year-old sailor swimming in the harbor at Havana, Cuba. In the first attack, the boy lost the flesh of his right leg from the calf down. In the second attack, the rogue shark bit off Brook's foot. His shipmates were near him in a skiff (small boat). They used a boat hook to drive away the shark, which tried to attack the boy a third time. A surgeon saved his life, amputating the leg below the knee, and he lived the rest of his life with a wooden leg.

Case closed? Brook Watson did not exactly fade away into history. That year the account inspired artist John Singleton Copley of Boston, Massachusetts, to paint several versions of the shark attack. Three of them hang in major US art museums, including the National Gallery in Washington, DC, the Metropolitan Museum of Art in New York City, and the Museum of Fine Art in Boston. The painting contributed to centuries of

American artist John Singleton Copley (1738–1815) painted *Watson and the Shark* in 1778. With its realistic depiction of a grisly shark attack, the painting was a sensation. Copley became very wealthy selling engravings based on the work.

fear of sharks. It shows Brook, floundering belly-up, eyes rolled back in his head, before a horrifying shark so large it dwarfs his boat.

SUMMER FIERCER THAN OTHERS

Skip forward to the beginning of the twentieth century, when many Americans had more leisure time than in previous centuries. They began to take shore vacations in greater numbers than ever. A few shark bites on the New Jersey shore of the Atlantic Ocean got major press attention and caused a panic. During World War II (1939–1945), an enemy German U-boat sank the USS *Indianapolis*. Newspaper headlines about sharks hunting down survivors gripped the nation. In the early twenty-first century, *Time* magazine used a series of summer shark attacks in 2001 to lure readers. The magazine's Summer of the Shark coverage ensured readership during a season with few hard-news events. The magazine focused on rare but frightening shark attacks. For example, on July 6, 2001, at dusk, a 7-foot (2.1 m) bull shark attacked eight-year-old Jesse Arbogast in shallow water off the coast of Pensacola, Florida. The boy's uncle wrestled the shark to shore and, with the help of a park ranger, retrieved the boy's severed arm from the shark's mouth. The boy was rushed to a nearby hospital where surgeons reattached his arm. He survived.

Then, in September, on Labor Day weekend that year, a sandbar shark bit a ten-year-old boy on the leg while he was surfing off Virginia Beach, Virginia. The same weekend, another shark (likely a bull or tiger shark) attacked a young man and woman while they were wading in the ocean off Avon, North Carolina. Both later died.

And yet, even though the attacks in 2001 were horrifying, the number of shark attacks worldwide was actually *down* to seventy-six, eleven fewer than the eighty-five attacks the previous year. Globally, five people died from shark bites in 2001, while twelve had died the year before.

A CHANGE OF HEART— AND HISTORY

Peter Benchley, who made the shark-scare films *Jaws*, *Beast*, and *The Deep* along with documentaries about sharks, said Americans in the twentieth century perceived shark attacks to be occurring more frequently. However, the real explanation was that more people were living near the shore and swimming in the water. So their exposure to sharks and the risk of encounters were increasing. Improved communications also helped spread stories—and panic. Shark attacks leveled off in the 1990s to sixty to eighty attacks a year worldwide.

SHARK TRUTH

Humans fear sharks as scary predators. Yet in the shark world, humans are the scary predators. Sharks have no other predator. Rarely will orca (killer whales), sperm whales, large bony fish such as groupers, and other sharks go after sharks.

A scuba diver and snorkeler, Benchley swam with sharks of all species all over the world. He was threatened, bumped, and shoved but never attacked or bitten. "I couldn't possibly write the same story today," Benchley said in his 2002 book *Shark Life*. "I know now that the mythic monster I created [the shark in *Jaws*] was largely a fiction. The genuine animal is just as—if not even more—fascinating."

When Benchley wrote *Shark Life*, conservationists and the public weren't advocating for sharks the way they were for other marine animals. Benchley said, "Whales and dolphins are easy to study and easier still to love." He said this is because dolphins and whales are mammals, like humans. Like us, they breathe air, nurture their young, learn tricks, and are smart. They respond to humans and seem to like us. Sharks, on the other hand, are fish. They don't share human traits and don't seem very interested in us. And they don't come up for air the way whales and dolphins do. So sharks are harder to see, track, and count.

Sharks also have the reputation of chomping people. "It's hard to care deeply for something that might turn on you and eat you," Benchley said. But just how often does that really happen?

STAYING OUT OF THE SHARK'S FOOD CHAIN

Most sharks avoid contact with humans. Alison Kock is a marine biologist and shark expert with the Cape Research Centre (South African National Parks) in Cape Town, South Africa. According to Kock, the sharks that are most likely to attack humans are the great white, bull, and tiger sharks. Key to avoiding attack, she says, is to recognize that sharks don't show up just anywhere. They follow predictable patterns of migration and hunt in areas where they are likely to find prey. Avoid those areas. Pay attention to any alert systems in place, such as signs and flags. And be aware that these big sharks are stealthy. Like lions, tigers, and other apex (top) predators, they sneak up on prey without warning.

Here are a few suggestions for protecting yourself from sharks:

- **RECOGNIZE THAT YOU ARE ENTERING SHARK TERRITORY WHEN YOU GO SWIMMING IN AN OCEAN**. Sharks don't specifically target people, but people do resemble shark prey—especially seals. This is true whether you are swimming, surfing, or kayaking.
- **DON'T SWIM ALONE**. Stay near the shore. Don't swim at dawn or dusk, when sharks are most likely to be hunting.
- **WHEN ENTERING THE WATER, LOOK FOR CUES—SUCH AS BIRDS DIVING FOR FISH OR FISHING BOATS HAULING IN THEIR CATCH—THAT SHARKS MIGHT BE IN THE WATER**. If there's food in the water, sharks may be hunting it, just as the birds and people are.
- **IF YOU ARE SCUBA DIVING AND YOU SEE A SHARK, STAY CALM AND PAY ATTENTION TO YOUR OXYGEN TANK**. Fear and anxiety can cause you to breathe too quickly and use up vital oxygen.
- **KNOW AND LOOK FOR THE BEHAVIORS THAT INDICATE A SHARK IS ABOUT TO ATTACK**. It will usually circle nearer to its prey and then swim straight toward it. At the last instant, the nictitating membrane (inner eyelid) may cover the shark's eye to protect it during the attack.
- **MYTHS ABOUND ABOUT HOW TO REPEL A SHARK ATTACK, BUT PUNCHING A SHARK IN THE NOSE OR PLAYING DEAD DON'T ACTUALLY WORK TOO WELL**. (And it is hard to do either one underwater.) What may work is poking the shark in the eye, one of its vulnerable points.
- **ABOVE ALL, DON'T BE A JERK AROUND SHARKS**. Human behavior provokes more than half of all shark attacks. Even the most peaceable sharks, such as whale sharks and nurse sharks, may bite if someone grabs them by the tail. Don't try to wrestle with or ride a shark. These types of thoughtless behaviors scare sharks and make them think their lives are at risk.

WHO'S ATTACKING WHOM?

George H. Burgess and Lindsay French of the Museum of Natural History at the University of Florida in Gainesville maintain the International Shark Attack File. This is a case-by-case study of interactions between humans and sharks.

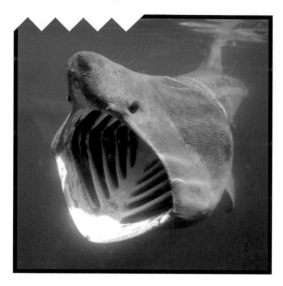

Basking sharks keep their mouths open while they swim. Through their many rows of tiny teeth, they filter plankton (small marine creatures) from the water to eat. The population of these sharks is declining. The animal's survival is at risk, mostly due to overfishing and very slow rates of population recovery.

In 2016 they counted 150 human-shark interactions worldwide. Of these, 81 were unprovoked attacks, in which people weren't fishing or doing anything else to put themselves at risk. Four people died from these attacks. Boris Worm, a marine research ecologist at Dalhousie University in Halifax, Nova Scotia, points out that humans kill a "staggering" number of sharks—one hundred million—each year, possibly more than twice that number. By fall 2016, the Convention on International Trade in Endangered Species of Wild Fauna and Flora (CITES) had listed seventeen shark species—including the silky, great white, whale, basking, and smooth hammerhead shark—on Appendix II. This document lists shark species that may not survive without efforts to control shark hunting.

FAME AND INFAMY

Nonetheless, shark attacks, both real and imagined, have led humans to exact vengeance over the centuries on the large fish. Many people didn't care much what happened to sharks and took actions that reflected their own shuddering horror. For example, the government of Western Australia began shark culls in 2014. In these outings, people use baited lines or nets to capture and kill sharks that are near beaches or that have bitten people. University of Sydney (Australia) public policy researcher Christopher Neff described the hunters' assumption. They believe that sharks mean to bite humans, that a shark bite is always fatal, and that once a shark has bitten a person, it must be killed to stop it from killing again. None of these beliefs is true. In the United States, attitudes supported by scary shark stories in the news and entertainment have sparked shark-hunting tournaments that reflect a human wish for good (humans) to conquer evil (sharks).

Sharks may seem bad, horrible, and terrifying. Yet they are truly fascinating, with a major role to play in worldwide food chains, and they spend their lives doing that. If they harm people, it is usually by accident, not with evil intent. In the mid-twentieth century, Eugenie Clark helped shift the way people think of sharks. Clark was a pioneer as a woman scientist and as an ichthyologist (a shark scientist). Her 1953 international best seller, *Lady with a Spear*, tells of her graduate work studying sharks in Indonesia. Clark founded a shark laboratory in Sarasota, Florida, that would became the Mote Marine

SHARK TRUTH

Florida has the most shark attacks of any state and the largest portion (40 percent) of shark attacks in the world. This is because Florida has many ocean beaches that large numbers of people, including surfers, use. The waters there also have large numbers of sharks.

A personal narrative of ten years of adventure and scientific experiments with sharks, manta rays and many smaller creatures by the founder of Florida's Cape Haze Marine Laboratory.

The LADY and the SHARKS
Eugenie Clark
author of LADY WITH A SPEAR

World-renowned ichthyologist Eugenie Clark (1922–2015) became interested in fish when she was a little girl in New York City. When visiting the New York Aquarium, she would think about what it would be like to be inside the shark tank swimming with the animals. From there, she went on to be a pioneer in marine conservation, scuba diving for research purposes, and shark behavior. She wrote two popular books, *Lady with a Spear* (1953) and *The Lady and the Sharks* (1969).

French marine explorer Jacques Cousteau, and his vessel the *Calypso*, became famous in the United States for his popular television show *The Undersea World of Jacques Cousteau*. The show ran for several seasons, from 1968 until 1976. Narrated by famous screenwriter Rod Sterling, the documentary show focused on the diversity of aquatic life, from sharks and whales to sea otters and penguins.

Laboratory, still an important center of shark research. She discovered a natural shark repellent—a secretion from flatfish that sharks avoid. She also studied shark intelligence. Clark's work became the subject of intriguing articles in *National Geographic*, and in the 1960s, she found an ally. Jacques Cousteau, a French oceanographer who was about to become a big TV star, joined her as another committed force working for sharks.

In 1968 the first episode of a television show called *The Undersea World of Jacques Cousteau* captured the public's imagination. Cousteau, a diver and underwater photographer, and his team placed tracking tags on sharks and then tailed them with cameras to trace their migration paths. For the first time, the public got a glimpse of what sharks did. And they got a look at the scientists in their sleek wet suits, flippers, and scuba gear as they studied the marine animals. As viewers got a clearer look at the sea and its sharks (which did not make meals of the Cousteau team), another vision of sharks began to emerge.

BLOCKBUSTERS WITH BITE

Gradually people began to gain another perspective on the shark story: peaceable sharks going about their business. In 1988 the brand-new Discovery Channel launched Shark Week, an education program, scheduled during the dog days of summer. The producers had noticed that the channel's ratings bumped up sharply whenever they aired a show about sharks. So why not a whole week of programs about sharks? Shark Week proved to be so popular that it still airs every summer. High-definition video cameras now allow audiences to get to know individual sharks. Storytelling from shark experts also reveals a more realistic, less horror-driven shark tale. Partly because of Shark Week and scientists such as Clark and Cousteau, public attitudes have changed toward a more humane and realistic understanding of sharks.

AUMAKUA: GIVING AND TAKING LIFE

Indigenous (native) Hawaiian mythology honors sharks. For example, several gods and goddesses take the form of a shark. This shark protects humans from shark attacks and may even carry shipwreck victims to safety. After a death, traditional indigenous Hawaiian families might ask a kahuna (spiritual or magical guide) to send the spirit of a dead loved one into the body of a guardian shark called an aumakua.

Some families teach their children to feed and protect the aumakua. In one ceremony, a young person will give the first fish they have caught to a shark and scrape the barnacles off the shark's back as a service to it. In return, some families believe the aumakua will chase fish into their fishing net and chase off other sharks. Carol Silva, a researcher of native Hawaiian culture, says that in the indigenous Hawaiian worldview, "Sharks are powerful. They have the ability to harm and take life. But they also have the ability to give life."

BAD NEWS FOR SHARKS

One of the most vital pieces of the shark puzzle is population. How many sharks live in the ocean? Another key piece is distribution. Where do they live? In 2003 Julia Baum, Ransom Myers, and other biologists at Dalhousie University published a headline-making study. It revealed shocking reductions in the population of sharks in the northwestern Atlantic Ocean. Their study showed that the main cause for fewer sharks is fishing. Since the 1960s, commercial fishing has relied on longlining—baiting hooks on lines that are miles long (some more than 40 miles, or 64 km). Fishing boats with long lines can go far out in the open ocean to catch tuna, swordfish, and other food fish. Bycatch (accidental hooking) is a risk for sharks, however, and longliners keep track of it. In some areas of the ocean, 90 percent of

Deep-sea fishing fleets that rely on long, hooked lines to catch fish at sea often accidentally hook sharks. Millions of bycatch sharks die every year because once hooked (or caught in nets), they can no longer swim. Swimming is necessary for oxygen to move into the animal's body, and the animals therefore suffocate. Many sharks die even after they are released. Some longliners are shifting away from wire lines to a monofilament that sharks can bite through to escape if hooked.

all longline captures are sharks. Drift gill nets, designed to entangle fish, also snare sharks. And millions of sharks die when they are tangled in other fishing gear. Others die through more direct, irresponsible fishing practices when fishers target the animals for just one body part, usually their fins.

The Dalhousie team wrote, "We estimate that all recorded shark species, with the exception of makos, have declined by more than 50% in the past 8 to 15 years." For some species, the statistics were far worse. From 1985 to 2000, hammerhead shark stocks declined by 89 percent, white sharks by 79 percent, tiger sharks by 75 percent, and threshers by 70 percent. The study reflected a global trend. In 2003 CITES for the first time placed four shark species—basking sharks, whale sharks, great white sharks, and sawfish—on its Appendix II.

Besides fishing, pollution harms sharks. Plastic pollution gets into their systems as water passes through their gills. Microplastics in the water— microscopic or hard-to-see pellets and pieces of plastic bottles, bags, and other trash—are left behind in sharks' guts. Plastic is persistent. It breaks down extremely slowly and is almost impossible to eradicate. So are certain persistent organic pollutants (POPs), such as pesticides and industrial chemicals. Animals at the top of the food chain, like sharks, accumulate high concentrations of POPs over a lifetime of eating smaller fish that also have the pollutants in their bodies. Other invisible pollution hurts too. Noise from ocean-based industries and construction travels at the low frequencies to which sharks are sensitive. Scientists are working to assess the effect noise pollution has on sharks of different species and habitats.

And the ocean has natural substances that may suddenly strike down particular animals. These substances include bacteria and parasites that have caused infections at an epidemic level among sharks. In recent years, leopard sharks have washed up, stranded, on beaches in San Francisco Bay. California Department of Fish and Wildlife fish pathologist Mark Okihiro examined the bodies. He found infections, likely caused by a fungus, in the sharks' brains. California State University shark biologist Chris Lowe says that without more funding for research, the infection could go global.

Shark fins are a specialty item in many Asian cuisines. Commercial fishing fleets usually haul the sharks on board, where they cut off the fins while the animal is still alive. Then they throw the sharks back into the ocean, where they bleed to death, suffocate, or are eaten by other sea animals. Processors remove the denticles from the fins, bleach the fins, and then dry, freeze, or cook them for sale.

FINS AS FOOD

The commercial trade in shark fins, meat, cartilage, skin, oil, and other shark products have further reduced the ocean's shark population. Shark fin soup is a delicacy in China and other Asian nations. A shark's fin is made of long, narrow fibers called ceratotrichia. Fins have no taste, but the fibers give them a silky, chewy texture that makes the soup desirable. One bowl of shark fin soup may sell for as much as $100. What's more, shark fins keep well (dry or frozen) for a long time. Every year commercial fishers strip seventy-three million sharks of their fins and throw the animals back into the water, often alive, for the sake of this soup. Sharks cannot regrow their fins, and without them, the animals will die by bleeding, drowning, or attack from killer whales and other predators.

According to the US Shark Conservation Act of 2010, all sharks caught in US waters must be brought to shore intact (with all their fins). Other countries are working to regulate shark finning as well. However, shark fin soup is a tradition in China, where hosts serve the soup to show guests respect or to demonstrate their own prestige, and change is slow.

From Asia and East Africa to western Europe and the United States, people have eaten shark meat for centuries. In some parts of the world, people use the meat and skin as medicine. Shark meat may be eaten and stored fresh, chilled, frozen, or salted and smoked or dried. Those with a taste for shark say the best meat comes from shortfin mako, porbeagle, and common thresher sharks.

Commercial fishing is devastating shark populations, however. Depending on the shark species, the animal's reproduction cycle is long. Sharks don't reach mating age until they are at least seven years old, some not until fifteen. Shark gestation periods (pregnancies) last two to three years. Some females give birth to small litters of only two young, while others may have up to eighty young. Recreational fishers put sharks at risk too. They catch and kill large sharks such as porbeagle, shortfin mako, and thresher for sport. Changes to their habitats due to pollution, warming waters from climate change, and disruption from commercial shipping and industries such as gas exploration also affect sharks.

Twenty-first-century shark seekers are using social media, smartphones, and good storytelling to improve the planet for this animal. The lead characters in the stories are only occasionally threatening. They are always awe-inspiring.

2
WHAT'S A SHARK?

YOU'RE BIGGER THAN ME, AND MORE POWERFUL. YOU'RE THE PRODUCT OF 450 MILLION YEARS OF EVOLUTION, AND YOU ARE, AS SHARKS GO, PERFECT. YOU WIN.

—SHARK WEEK EXECUTIVE PRODUCER BROOKE RUNNETTE,
IN AN IMAGINED CONVERSATION WITH A GREAT WHITE SHARK,
IN AN ARTICLE IN THE *ATLANTIC*, 2012

Sharks with red frills and tiger stripes. Sharks with saw-shaped snouts and scythe-shaped tails. Tiny sharks and monster sharks. No matter the color, shape, or size, all sharks are cartilaginous fishes, a biological class called Chondrichthyes. The fish family has two main forks, bony fish and the class Osteichthyes, to which sharks belong. Instead of scales, sharks have skin. Instead of bone, their skeletons are made of cartilage, a tough, flexible material like that of human ears or the tips of our noses. The shark family tree includes twelve branches—three for extinct sharks, eight for living sharks, and one branch for rays and skates.

Anguineus, the species name of the frilled shark (*Chlamydoselachus anguineus*), means "snaky" in Latin. It refers to the animal's long snakelike body. *C. anguineus*'s common name—frilled shark—refers to the red, frilly fringe that lines the edges of the shark's gills. The shark has three hundred backward-facing, fork-shaped teeth arranged in twenty-five rows. The shark has changed little since prehistoric times.

Scientists know of five hundred species of sharks swimming in all the world's oceans. As marine researchers dive deeper and investigate further, they are finding even more. For example, in 1976 a crew on a US Navy ship off Hawaii discovered a new shark species called the megamouth. That may seem like a long time ago. But if this large plankton-eating shark (up to 18 feet, or 5.5 m) could keep out of sight for so long, how many species of small, pelagic (open ocean), deep-dwelling sharks may yet be discovered?

Commercial fishing fleets and recreational anglers are discovering new shark species too. Citizen scientists of all stripes are helping with shark research. They include recreational fishers, scuba divers, snorkelers, beachcombers, and others who may find useful evidence in their own watery backyards. With new technologies, citizens are tracking sharks with their smartphones. And some of those who are good at catching sharks have reeled them in for tagging.

OLD AS THE HILLS

All life, including sharks, originated in the sea. Icthyologists have fossil evidence that sharks evolved about 420 million years ago. That's before dinosaurs, before birds, and even before some mountains. Shark fossils are among the most abundant and enduring fossils. Paleontologists (scientists who study the remains of once-living creatures) have found ancient shark teeth

Squalicorax, or the crow shark, is best known for its distinctive teeth. From fossilized teeth such as this one viewers can see the shark tooth's rectangular root at the base. The tooth itself has finely serrated (notched) edges.

all over the world. One ancient shark, nicknamed Squalicorax, or the "crow shark," was a scavenger that fed on carrion (dead animals). Researchers found a 6-foot (1.8 m) fossilized specimen in Kansas, where it died more than sixty-five million years ago. Were there really such things as land sharks? Sort of . . .

Kansas once formed the bed of an immense inland sea. How do scientists know the shark lived on carrion? Paleontologist David Schwimmer found Squalicorax teeth embedded in the fossilized foot bones of a hadrosaurus, a duck-billed, land-based dinosaur. The Squalicorax diet is like that of the modern tiger shark. Nicknamed the wastebasket of the sea, the tiger shark has a wider-ranging diet than sea snakes, dolphins, and other sharks.

Shark fossils also indicate that more than three thousand shark species have become extinct. Researchers believe that many more species also became extinct. Scientists disagree on the number of evolutionary links that

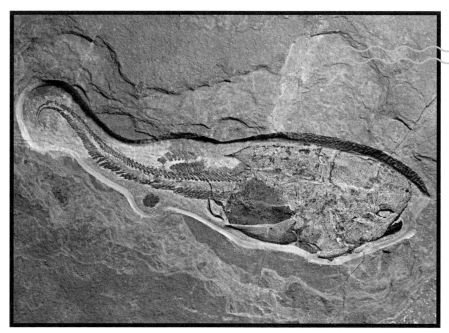

This placoderm fossil was found in Scotland. Placoderms, from which sharks evolved, are the earliest known branch of jawed fishes. They had heavy and bony armorlike plates on the head and neck.

connect ancient sharks to modern sharks. For example, some researchers say *Carcharodon megalodon*, a 50-foot (15 m) shark that lived about thirty million years ago, is the direct ancestor of the great white shark. Others say the mako shark is *Carcharodon*'s true descendant.

Even with these disagreements, scientists think sharks most likely evolved from placoderms, a group of now-extinct armored bony fishes. Scientists consider the animals to be highly evolved since they have changed little over the last one hundred million years. This indicates that sharks have long been well adapted to their environment. Key to the success of this adaptation are the biting jaws that ichthyologists think developed from skeletal arches supporting shark gills. (In contrast, bony fish have a stationary upper jaw that is part of their skull.) Early shark ancestors were slow swimmers, but once they developed paired fins (one on each side of the body), their swimming speed increased dramatically. The combination of swimming speed—sharks can swim more than 31 miles (50 km) per hour—and big strong jaws put sharks on the path to becoming eating machines.

NICHE AND NOSH

Each individual shark species has adapted over generations to weed out weak traits and to select for (reproduce) special features and abilities that promote survival. These shark superpowers help sharks fit into what natural historians call a niche, or a position in the food chain. A niche is a source of food, shelter, or environment. But it's available only if a species has the physical equipment or the moves (the wits or behaviors) to take advantage of it.

You might say nosh (food) dictates niche. Over their evolutionary history, sharks have developed teeth, senses, swimming skills, and hunting behaviors that are uniquely suited to find, catch, and eat the food that is available in their niche. These adaptations range from behavior, such as how far sharks will migrate, to physical attributes that allow them to make the most of their ocean environment.

Some sharks, like the blue shark, migrate across entire oceans. Icthyologists tag sharks with devices that communicate the animals' positions by satellite. The devices show that great white sharks make annual migrations that take them from the Atlantic coast of New England southward beyond the Florida Keys off the southeastern tip of Florida. If sharks swam in a straight path, which they don't, this would be a round-trip of more than 3,000 miles (4,828 km). So the great white shark journey is actually longer.

While certain species of sharks dwell in the icy waters of the far north and south, most prefer warm tropical waters near the equator. Others like cooler waters farther from the equator. Sharks like a range of depths, from shallow-water sharks, coastal sharks, pelagic sharks, and benthic (seafloor) sharks. Most sharks live in waters a little more than 300 feet (91 m) deep.

Greenland sharks live at depths of 1.4 miles (2.3 km) in the Arctic and North Atlantic oceans. In 2017 Danish scientists discovered a Greenland shark they believe may be at least five hundred years old.

Deeper divers include dogfish, some catsharks, the Greenland shark, the kitefin shark, the sand devil, and the great lanternshark, which may dive 3,000 feet (914 m). Certain species, including the bull shark, will venture from salt water to brackish water (part salt, part fresh) all the way inland to freshwater.

Bony fish have a swim bladder that allows them to maintain the neutral buoyancy they need to swim—neither sinking nor bobbing up to the top. Sharks use their large livers to stay at their desired depth. The livers hold a lot of natural oil, called squalene. Big sharks may produce as much as 550 gallons (2,082 L) of squalene! How does an oily liver translate into buoyancy? Water is denser and therefore heavier than the oil in sharks' livers. So, with large livers holding a lot of lighter oil, the shark itself weighs a lot less than the surrounding water and will stay afloat. Certain pelagic sharks also have a snout with deposits of jelly that are lighter than water. This helps them stay even higher at their optimum depth in the ocean's water column.

Shark cartilage also naturally promotes buoyancy. Cartilage is light and flexible. (Check the difference between the cartilage in your nose and the bone in your cheek.) Cartilage is lighter than bone, so in relation to their size, sharks weigh less than bony fish of similar size.

IT'S ALL ABOUT SHAPE

Most sharks have a streamlined body. They have a long, flattened snout and a ventral parabolic mouth. This type of mouth, shaped like an upside-down U or a rounded V, is on the ventral (front) side of the head. Most sharks have an asymmetrical caudal (tail) fin whose upper lobe is much longer than the lower one. A thresher shark's upper tail lobe, for example, is almost as

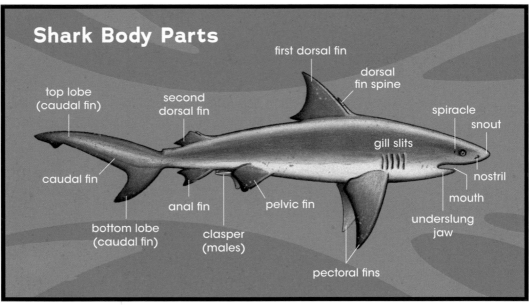

Shark morphology (shape and structure of the body) is all about moving efficiently through the water. Sharks are also well equipped to eat a variety of marine creatures from tiny plankton to big whales.

long as its body. The shark whips its tail to stun small food fish. Like bony fish, sharks have gills, pairs of organs on the sides of their heads or throats that draw oxygen out of the water as it flows through them.

Head, trunk, and tail are the essential sections of a shark. The five hundred (or more) shark species known to swim the world's oceans show mind-boggling variations of these parts. Most shark species are small, less than 59 inches (150 cm) long from the tip of the snout to the tip of the tail. Yet sharks can be as massive as the 66-foot (20 m) whale shark or as tiny as the tiniest lanternshark, just 1 foot long (30 cm) when fully grown. Sharks may live and swim at the surface of the ocean, in its deepest trenches, or at any depth in between. They may eat whales three times as big as their own bodies, or they may eat only tiny plankton.

BORN THIS WAY

Body shapes vary depending on habitat. The chain catshark, for example, is long and slender so it can hunt prey along the rocky bottoms. The sand devil (also benthic) has a flat, compressed body. The pelagic shortfin mako is shaped like a spindle—narrow in front and back and rounder in the middle. This sleek shape gives the shark its record-breaking speed. Shortfin makos are the fastest sharks, with maximum speeds of more than 46 miles (74 km) per hour.

A shark's fins aid in propulsion (forward movement), stability, and steering. Most sharks have eight fins: two pectoral (ventral forward/underbody), two pelvic (ventral middle), first dorsal (the big forward fin on the shark's back), second dorsal (middle fin on the back), one anal (ventral rear), and one caudal fin (tail). Some sharks have fewer or reduced fins. For example, dogfish sharks have no anal fin. Shark fins are made of cartilage and are less flexible than fish fins. Bony fish fins have umbrella-like spines that help the fins expand and contract. They also have muscles for folding their fins. This flexibility allows fish to hover and to swim backward. Lacking these same spines and muscles, sharks are not as agile. They only swim forward and don't hover the way bony fish can.

This scanning electron microscope view of the dermal denticles of a great white shark reveal the texture and the channels in the shark's skin. Together the features allow the shark to move hydrodynamically through water.

Among the other ways in which sharks differ from bony fish are these:

- **JAW STRUCTURE**. Bony fish have two bone jaws. Sharks have one jaw made of cartilage.
- **EYELIDS**. Fish don't have them, but sharks do.
- **REPRODUCTIVE SYSTEMS AND METHODS**. Most fish lay eggs, which are fertilized or mature outside their bodies. Many sharks mate and have live young.
- **SKIN**. Fish are smooth, with scales. Sharks have rough skin.

Most people know that (bony) fish have scales. But sharks have dermal (skin-based) denticles, or tooth-shaped placoid pieces. The word *placoid* refers to the enamel that coats the denticles. This enamel is like the enamel or plaque on human teeth. And a shark's denticles really are like mouth-based teeth, with enamel crowns and sockets just like the ones in which human teeth are anchored. Sharkskin allows the animals to move fast. The ridges in the denticles line up to form water channels that cut down on drag.

IDENTIFYING SHARKS

Icthyologists use a number of different features to identify the type of shark they are observing. They include these:

- **BODY SHAPE AND LENGTH.** Angel sharks, for example, have a flattened body.
- **SHAPE OF SNOUT.** Hammerhead sharks (*below*) have a snout that is shaped, you guessed it, like a hammer.
- **PRESENCE OF SPIRACLES, SMALL GILL SLITS JUST BEHIND THE EYES.** Angel sharks have these.
- **SIZE AND COLOR OF EYES.** Bigeye threshers have, you guessed it, big eyes.
- **NUMBER, SIZE, AND POSITION OF GILL SLITS.** Most sharks have five gills. Some, like the bigeyed six-gill sharks, have more.
- **TEETH.** Sand tigers, for example, have teeth that protrude from the mouth.
- **SHAPE AND POSITION OF FINS, AND THE PRESENCE OF DORSAL AND ANAL FINS.** Bramble sharks, for example, have no anal fin.
- **COLOR AND PATTERN OF SKIN.** Shortfin makos, for example, are a deep purple.

Sharks come in many colors—usually shades of brown, gray, blue, and green. Viewed from the top, these colors blend in with the seafloor and with vegetation, waters beneath the animals, or both. Viewed from beneath, a shark's white belly is perfect camouflage against the brightly lit surface of the water. Spotty skin patterns add to the camouflage for sand tigers and Greenland sharks. The white tips of the fins of whitetip sharks resemble sparkling food fish—attracting the fish's predators (bigger fish) to the whitetip's attack range.

SHARK TRUTH

Albino sharks are rare. Albinism (the absence of coloration) occurs in great white, basking, leopard, sandbar, tiger, whitespotted bamboo, and some other sharks. Young porbeagle and mako sharks are white, which sometimes causes people to misidentify them as albinos. Most albino sharks are embryos or newborns. They don't live long because they make easy targets for prey animals.

BLOOD AND BREATH

Sharks have evolved to fill niches with different temperatures as well as different foods. Like fish and other cold-blooded creatures, most sharks have a variable body temperature that matches the temperature of their environment. Certain sharks can heat their bodies—and blood—to a temperature higher than the surrounding water. This ability, called endothermy (inner heating), allows shortfin makos, great whites, threshers, and other strong, speedy sharks to process food into muscle energy very quickly. Red muscle cells that maintain a warmer temperature than the surrounding water keep sharks' brains and eyes warm so they can react quickly. These sharks are faster and more powerful than other shark species. These are the sharks of Internet fame that shoot out of the water to grab a leaping fish or seal.

Sharks rely on their gills for breathing. Respiration is also a factor in speed. Say you are a fast-moving shark, such as the blue shark or the mako.

You need a lot of oxygen to move quickly, you need it fast, and you don't want to waste a lot of energy to get it. So these sharks have adapted to swim forward quickly with their mouths open. Through the force of the forward movement, oxygen-rich water rushes into their mouths and quickly out through their gills. Oxygen from that water remains inside the shark's body. Scientists refer to this adaptation as ram ventilation, since these sharks get their air by literally ramming into and through it.

But what if you're a bottom lurker that needs to stay still and stealthy to capture prey while breathing at the same time? Certain sharks have six or seven gills instead of the usual five. Others (like the endothermic makos) have extra-long gills that let them take in more oxygen in one gulp. And some sneaky sharks that hide in the sand have developed spiracles, small

Most sharks, such as this thresher, have five pairs of gills, one set on each side of the head. Water (which contains oxygen) must flow over the gills for the shark to breathe. So the animal must be swimming or, in some cases, such as with the nurse shark, using its fins to fan water over the gills.

round openings near their eyes. Spiracles let water pass through the body to the gills from above so the shark can breathe while it is lying on the seafloor.

Scientists once thought that sharks would die if they stopped swimming. Water would no longer pour through their gills, and they would suffocate from lack of oxygen. In 1972 free diver Ramón Bravo led marine biologist Eugenie Clark to a water-filled cave in Mexico's Yucatán Peninsula. Bravo showed her a group of sleeping Caribbean reef sharks, disproving the theory that sharks die if they stop moving.

Then there is the frilled shark. This prehistoric-looking, rarely seen, deep-dwelling shark has a snake-shaped body and three hundred teeth in twenty-five rows. Its long red-frilled gills extend from the sides down to its throat. (The gills of most sharks are shorter and farther back.) These gills give the shark its common name. Its Latin species name, *anguineus*, means "snaky." The frilled shark has dermal denticles not only on its outer skin but

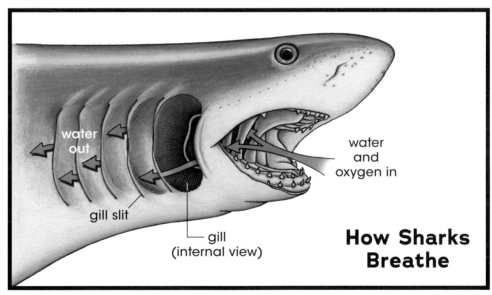

water out

water and oxygen in

gill slit

gill (internal view)

How Sharks Breathe

Most of the ocean's water contains oxygen. Sharks take the oxygen out of the water to breathe. To do this, water is drawn into a shark's mouth and is passed over its gills. As the water flows over the gills' many small blood vessels, oxygen is transferred from the water into the shark's blood. Finally, the water flows out of the shark's gill slits.

also inside its mouth. Unchanged for millions of years, this shark has exactly what it needs to flourish in its deep-ocean niche.

Adaptations aren't always obvious. Sharks can surprise experts when they observe that the fish are handling conditions outside the habitat to which scientists *thought* they had best adapted. During a 2014 live broadcast from aboard the research ship *Exploration Vessel Nautilus*, viewers around the world watched the video feed from the cameras of *Hercules*, the ship's robotic submersible (underwater rover). *Hercules* recorded chain catsharks (named for the chain patterns on their skin) lying on the floor of the Gulf of Mexico, hundreds of feet deeper than they had ever been observed before.

Researchers are regularly discovering these and other new adaptations in the shark world. They are also discovering new shark species. The more we study sharks, the more astonishing we find their superpowers to be.

3
FEEDING THE BEAST

EVERYTHING ABOUT HIM WAS BEAUTIFUL EXCEPT HIS JAWS. . . . WHEN THE OLD MAN SAW HIM COMING HE KNEW THAT THIS WAS A SHARK THAT HAD NO FEAR AT ALL AND WOULD DO EXACTLY WHAT HE WISHED.

—ERNEST HEMINGWAY, *THE OLD MAN AND THE SEA*

Like most living beings, humans included, sharks are opportunists. Their biological goal is to stay well fed, safe, and physically strong long enough to reproduce and to produce enough offspring to maintain the long-term survival of their species.

Sharks eat every chance they get. Their ability to survive and thrive depends on how well they can use the food they snap up. It helps that they have a digestive tract wide enough to accommodate whole fish, big chunks of mammal meat, and whatever else they eat. A big stomach in which to store food helps too—as does an intestine that quickly digests the food for energy.

Great white sharks, such as this one off the coast of South Africa, are known to breach, or leap out of the water, to catch fast-moving prey such as seals. The sharks do not breach often because doing so requires a lot of energy. But when they do, they may reach speeds of 40 miles (64 km) per hour and leap 10 feet (3 m) into the air.

Try Googling these keywords, "things found in shark stomachs." You'll find lists of hard-to-believe items, including everything from a can of peas to a whole polar bear (in the stomach of a Greenland shark). Sharks have another superpower that makes them the survivors they are. They can evert their stomachs, turning them inside out when they eat something indigestible or that just rubs them the wrong way. Sharks can get rid of things they literally can't stomach.

"GANGSTERS OF THE DEEP"

When it comes to finding food, nobody does it better than sharks. What do sharks think as they find food, which takes up most of their time? Eugenie Clark's work put to rest the idea that sharks are like Bruce, the robotic shark star in *Jaws*. She said, "People generally thought that sharks are dumb eating machines. After some study, I began to realize that these 'gangsters' of the deep had gotten a bad rap." Clark trained sharks to push a button for food. From that experience, she concluded that sharks are intelligent, since they can be trained.

To find their food and to survive in the ocean, sharks have evolved shark sense—superpower observation and detection skills. Alison Kock, who studies great white sharks, finds sharks to be inquisitive. And curiosity is another measurement of intelligence. What's more, Kock's colleague Leonard Compagno, director of the Shark Research Institute in Princeton, New Jersey, says that great whites have a social order. Each shark takes a certain role in the pecking order. Sharks sometimes hunt in groups, a measure of cooperation and another sign of shark smarts. "Once, when there were several people on the boat, the great white looked each person in the eye, one by one, checking us out," Compagno told *Smithsonian* magazine. "They feed on large-brained social animals such as seals and dolphins, and to do this you have to operate on a level higher than [the] simple machine mentality of an ordinary fish."

SHARK SENSE

Humans have five senses: vision, hearing, smell, taste, and touch. Sharks have four senses. But don't be fooled into thinking that means they are clueless about their environment. For each sense, they have highly developed supersensitive sensors. Most sharks are nocturnal, swimming and hunting in the dark and resting during the daytime. The four shark-sensing superpowers help them track down food and detect prey whenever it's around.

PHOTORECEPTION (LIGHT SENSE AND VISION COMBINED)

Sharks see well. Their retinas, the light receptor in their eyes, have adapted so the animals can see well in whatever light is available—dark or bright. Some sharks see colors.

Many sharks, including tiger sharks, have a nictitating membrane (a third, translucent eyelid) in their eyes. This defense mechanism covers the eyeball and protects it from the sharp claws or teeth of struggling prey. The membrane is an extra fold of eyelid that slides up to expose only a slit of the

Some sharks, such as the blue shark (*above*), have a nictitating eyelid membrane. The shark can close this membrane to protect the eye when attacking prey. Sharks such as the great white, which do not have this third eyelid, roll back their pupils for protection instead.

shark's eye. When this happens, it is a sure sign that the shark is starting a bite. Great whites do not have nictitating membranes, so they roll their eyes backward to protect them while attacking prey.

CHEMORECEPTION (SMELL AND TASTE COMBINED)

This sense helps sharks detect chemical clues in the water. Sharks have nostrils in their snouts that lead to the olfactory bulb, an internal smell processor. Nasal barbels (flaps) hang from some sharks' snouts. (Look for them on bottom-dwellers.) The barbels touch or drag along the bottom of the seafloor to taste for and sense the vibrations of prey that might be hiding under sand or sediment. Taste receptors in a shark's mouth and pharynx (throat) offer more information when the shark takes a test bite.

This nurse shark rests on the sand in the shallow waters of the Bahamas National Shark Sanctuary in the West Atlantic Ocean. Its long nasal barbels hang from its top lip and help the shark sense prey under the sand.

MECHANORECEPTION (MOTION DETECTORS)

Sharks have vibration sensors along their sides, in their ears and snouts, and all over their bodies. The lateral line is a row of pressure sensors along the shark's sides and head. The sensors pick up motion through changes in pressure waves and water currents that come from whatever is moving in the water. Sharks process the information from different types of vibrations (such as the distressed thrashing of a hurt fish) to determine what to check out and what to ignore. Endolymphatic ducts, narrow channels in the shark's inner ear, also pick up motion. Touch receptors over the shark's whole body offer more clues about nearby movements. Certain sharks with poor vision, such as bull sharks, will even head-butt something to find out more about it before taking a bite.

ELECTRORECEPTION (ELECTRICAL CHARGES)

Can sharks really smell blood a mile (1.6 km) away? Can they really sense fear? Ichthyologists have shown that both of these popular ideas are myths. But sharks *can* sense a pounding heart, through electroreception sensing. To humans, electroreception seems like extrasensory perception (ESP), extra information we can't logically or physically sense. But sharks actually *do* have an extra sense.

Sharks can detect electricity from miles away using ampullae of Lorenzini. These tiny jelly-filled pores in the snout detect very weak electrical pulses, about one billionth of a volt per meter. But what kind of electricity are they homing in on? The pores pick up electricity generated by moving muscles or firing neurons (nerve cells) of fish or other prey. Seawater conducts this electricity quite nicely, sending it straight to the shark's ampullae of Lorenzini and to the brain. Hammerhead sharks are especially good at finding prey because the ventral (lower) surface of their bodies has an abundance of ampullae of Lorenzini. Besides locating prey, ampullae of Lorenzini may help sharks navigate the ocean by figuring out where they are. Earth's electromagnetic field is a skin of energy that circles the planet, with a different level of energy at every spot. Many animals with a magnetic sense, including sea turtles and birds, use this field to navigate. With their ampullae, sharks have this ability too.

Pores known as ampullae of Lorenzini help sharks such as this lemon shark sense electrical impulses associated with muscle movements in prey animals. The pores are on the underside of a shark's snout and near its nostrils. They are connected to long, jelly-filled tubes that lead to cells below the skin that sense electrical activity. The pores are named for a seventeenth-century Italian doctor, Stefano Lorenzini. In Latin, *ampullae* refers to "amphora," a type of oval, two-handled pot. In anatomy, *ampullae* refers to widened tubes, such as ear canals or the shark pore system.

THE SHARCTIC CIRCLE

Lamnids are a clan of sharks that includes great whites, porbeagles, and shortfin mako. They live in frigid Arctic waters in an area informally known as the Sharctic Circle. The word *lamnids* comes from Lamia, a queen-turned-demon from Greek mythology. *Porbeagle* comes from the words *porpoise* and *beagle*. The shark is built like a dog, with a rigid, sleek, tough body for speed and big eyes (*right*), the better for spotting prey.

All lamnids have hydrodynamic tails shaped like a teardrop or airfoil (the wings of an airplane). This streamlining allows them to swim in fast bursts and maintain high speed. The real secret to lamnid cold-water success is a blood circulation system they share with ichthyosaurs, marine dinosaurs that became extinct about ninety million years ago, and with tuna. (Tuna and sharks share an ancient ancestor, but tuna evolved along a different path from sharks.) The lamnid circulation system includes a large heart, high blood pressure, and a rete mirabile, or "miraculous net." This netlike arrangement of blood vessels allows the warm blood pumping out of the heart and through arteries to heat up the cold blood that is coming into the heart through the veins. The result is a body temperature that is 13°F to 18°F (7°C to 10°C) warmer than the surrounding water. This significant advantage helps the sharks tolerate water temperatures as cold as 36°F (2°C) and gives them an edge over cold-blooded competitors such as seals.

The adaptation is quite different from the strategies of other Arctic marine animals, including walruses, whales, and polar bears. These mammals have heavy layers of blubber (fat) for insulation. The Greenland shark, whose evolution took a different path from other lamnids, moves slowly to conserve energy. It can endure icy water as cold as 29°F (–1.8°C) and relies on a strong sense of chemoreception to target prey. A substance in the skin called trimethylamine N-oxide (TMAO) keeps the skin from freezing. It is also poisonous to predators, including humans. But people in Greenland figured out a work-around. After drying the shark's meat, it becomes nontoxic.

LIGHT: ANOTHER SUPER SENSE?

Do sharks glow in the dark? David Gruber, a scientist at Baruch College in New York City, dives with deep-dwelling sharks to learn more about them. He discovered that two species of catshark—the chain catshark (*Scyliorhinus rotifer*) and the swell shark (*Cephaloscyllium ventriosum*)—biofluoresce, or glow in the dark. They may use this ability to locate or communicate with other sharks that live in deep, dark waters.

In biofluorescence, molecules in an animal's body take in blue (high-energy) light and give it back as green or red (lower-energy) light. Humans can't see biofluorescence. Only fish and some other sea creatures, including certain stingrays (a relative of sharks), fish, and sea turtles, can see the glow. Gruber and his team realized that catsharks probably can see the biofluorescent green light as well as the blue light.

Why do sharks biofluoresce? To find out, Gruber's team built a shark's-eye camera, adding filters to let in green and blue light. Wearing scuba gear, the scientists dove in Scripps Canyon, a large underwater gorge near San Diego, California. Sure enough, glowing green sharks loomed out of the deep.

The camera found that different catshark species each shine with their own patterns. And the patterns also vary between males and females. "This work forces us to take a step out of the human perspective and start imagining the world through a shark's perspective," Gruber told *National Geographic*. His future work will involve a closer look at the messages catsharks send out through biofluorescence. He thinks the green glow helps them locate and attract mates and to lure food prey.

SHARK TRUTH

Great white sharks are the only sharks that spy-hop. Like whales, they raise their heads above the water to investigate the surface. When sharks spy-hop closer to shore, they sometimes scare seals. The seals flee toward the open sea for security, right into the sharks' clutches.

EATING

Sharks are carnivores (meat eaters). The meat they eat includes everything from the tiniest plankton and krill to clams and crabs, squid, octopus, seabirds, sea snakes, small fish, big fish, jellyfish, marine mammals such as dolphins and manatees, sea turtles, and even other sharks and their relatives, rays. Most sharks—but not all—prey on animals that are smaller than they are. Only a few, including tiger sharks and great whites, will attack live whales and other marine mammals. Most sharks will feed only on dead ones.

Each species of shark eats a particular type of food prey and has the physiology (body features) for stalking and catching it. This includes teeth, jaws, skin color, and attacking behaviors best suited to catching the prey animal. For example, a great white shark charges up to attack seals and sea lions from below. It stuns the prey with a shocking chomp, retreats, and waits for the prey to die of blood loss before returning to eat it. Some scientists say that if the first bite isn't tasty enough, the shark may not return to finish the meal.

A shortfin mako will swim in a figure eight, signaling that it is getting ready to attack. Other sharks bump and circle their prey. A speedy blue shark will swim through a school of squid or fish with its mouth wide open, eating whatever swims in.

Dogfish attack in groups like a pack of sharp-toothed dogs. (That's how they got their name.) Packs of dogfish sharks often number in the hundreds as they pursue mackerel, capelin, squid, jellyfish, and other prey. Even newborn spiny dogfish—at most 49 inches (124 cm) long when fully grown—will attack prey more than twice their size. Adults will go after orca and seals. The spiny dogfish gets its name from two sharp and poisonous spines in front of each dorsal fin. The shark may stab its prey with the spines to inject venom. Threshers use their big swooping tail fins to stun and confuse prey fish. The fish become confused, and the threshers can easily corral them, or round them up.

Bottom-feeders such as the horn shark hunt alone at night. They sometimes slurp down so many sea urchins that their teeth turn purple. Surface skimmers such as the basking shark open wide to let plankton swim in. And others, including the velvet belly shark, live in the deeps during the day and migrate up to the surface to feed on squid and fish at night.

Sharks don't eat that much—3 to 5 percent of their body weight per meal. They make the most of their opportunities, eating whatever is available in the waters and every day if they can. And, if necessary, many shark species can lay off the chow for a few weeks, living off the oil reserves in their large livers.

SHARK TEETH

As meat eaters, sharks are well equipped with mouths and teeth. The basking shark has the biggest mouth among sharks. With its 3-foot-wide (1 m) mouth, this shark is a sort of swimming vacuum cleaner, eating tiny surface-dwelling plankton. Like its fellow plankton eaters, the whale shark and megamouth shark, basking sharks are mammoth. Their multitude of

Megamouth sharks were first discovered in 1976, off the coast of Hawaii, and are rarely seen by humans. The deep-sea sharks have giant, bathtub-sized mouths, though they are the smallest of the filter-feeding sharks. Because they do not actively pursue prey, they are slow swimmers and their muscles are not well developed.

tiny teeth (up to one hundred per row) aren't for chomping prey. They function as a filter to sift out prey from each mouthful of water. The water flows out through the gills, and food stays in.

Like the basking shark, the great white shark has jaws that open extra wide. But the great white isn't after tiny plankton. It is after huge prey—usually a seal. The zebra bullhead shark's jaw is adapted to feed from the seabed. Other sharks, such as lemon sharks, have teeth shaped like daggers to hold onto fast-moving, thrashing prey. Sharks such as nurse sharks, which prey on smaller fish, have smaller mouths and teeth.

Over millions of years and many generations, sharks became efficient predators. For example, ancient sharks had mouths in front of their eyes and at the end of their snouts, like dogs, eagles, and other carnivorous animals. Modern sharks mainly have ventral mouths that are on the underside of their body. As a shark attacks, its jaws shift and jut, its snout turns, and it throws its whole head and powerful body into biting and ripping at its food prey.

Shark teeth are different from other meat-eater teeth. Instead of growing from sockets, like human or wolf teeth, shark teeth are set in rows of grooves. Sharks have two sets of teeth, functional teeth for the kill and replacement teeth to fill in for lost functional teeth. And sharks lose teeth while feeding, as often as every two days. They replace any lost tooth with a tooth from the next row. It's something like the way a vending machine works. Buy a granola bar, and as it drops into the tray below, another bar slides forward to fill the empty slot. Depending on species, a shark may have as many as fifteen replacement rows.

The shape and size of shark teeth help researchers and beachcombers identify the species of shark and the type of prey they eat. Big, triangular teeth come from sharks such as great whites that feed on seals and other marine mammals as well as on big fish. The shortfin mako's narrow, curved teeth are perfect for nabbing speedy, darting schooling fish. The houndshark's teeth line up like small white stones along the shark's jaw to form what looks like a pebbled lip. These teeth are just right for crushing

Shortfin mako have long, smooth-edged teeth. Those at the front of the jaw are curved for grasping fish prey, which they swallow whole.

crunchy crustaceans (for example, crabs and lobsters). Horn sharks have smooth, flat teeth that resemble human molars to break the exoskeletons (exterior skeletons) of crabs, mussels, and other shellfish. A sand tiger has spiky teeth for piercing and tearing the flesh of its prey.

Some sharks have teeth that change shape as they grow larger and shift from hunting smaller prey to hunting something bigger. For example, a small shortfin mako will have little, thin teeth for eating small fish when it is young. As the shortfin mako grows to adult size, its teeth become bigger and stronger so it can graduate to hunting swordfish and dolphins. Every shark has just the right set of teeth for the job!

4

SHARK **SEX**

AWWWW. SO CUTE SEEING A BABY WHITE.

—INSTAGRAM COMMENT ABOUT OCEARCH RESEARCHERS' PHOTO OF
CAPTURING, TAGGING, AND RELEASING A BABY GREAT WHITE SHARK

Imagine you're a bay scallop—a small shellfish living in the shallow Atlantic Ocean waters off the eastern coast of North Carolina. What are you scared of? The cow-nose ray, one of your main predators. You wouldn't mind if fewer cow-nose rays were around. But actually, more of them share your habitat than ever before. Why? Because the population of smooth hammerhead sharks that prey on cow-nose rays is declining fast.

Hammerheads are in trouble. Fishing fleets catch them to sell as food fish, and they sometimes reel them in as bycatch. According to the Census of Marine Life, shark numbers are down so low that cow-nose rays are all over the place. They are eating so many bay scallops that North Carolina has had to close down the scallop fishery that has thrived on its Atlantic coast since the early twentieth century.

All ecosystems have a food chain hierarchy, or ranking of prey and predators. At the top are big apex predators, such as sharks.

Atlantic cow-nose rays are recognizable by their notched brow. Females give live birth to one pup per delivery. The gestation period is about one year. Members of the class of vertebrates known as Chondrichthyes, rays are closely related to sharks.

In the middle are mesopredators, medium-size animals such as cow-nose rays. Mesopredators are both prey for apex animals and predators of smaller animals, such as bay scallops. Balanced populations of each type of animal—neither too many nor too few—keep an ecosystem healthy and strong. But if any of the animals are threatened and their numbers decline—such as those of the hammerhead shark—the ecosystem goes out of balance and gets wobbly and weak.

"As the top predator in the Atlantic, the white shark is like the wolf of the sea, helping to maintain ecological balance by feeding on prey such as seals—especially the weaker and less fit," says Robert Hueter, a scientist at the Mote Marine Laboratory in Florida. Sharks make the oceans healthier by weeding out weak, sick, and old animals. Without predators in an ecosystem, one species may take over and a cascade of imbalance flows from there. For example, on coral reefs where hammerhead sharks are overfished, hammerhead prey such as snappers are becoming too abundant.

The mesopredators are therefore eating more of the smaller herbivorous (plant-eating) fish such as parrotfish that are below them in the food chain. Without parrotfish to feed on the algae that live on the coral, the algae population balloons. The algae then start to take up too much of the oxygen the coral needs to survive.

THE NEXT GENERATION

For all the trouble that sharks have turned to their advantage over their long evolutionary history, they didn't factor in humans. And when humans interact with sharks—mostly through fishing—they aren't factoring in the shark reproduction cycle. Sharks live on average twelve to twenty-seven years. That's nowhere near as long as a whale, which may live two hundred years. But it's much longer than the life of the average bony fish. Take swordfish, for example—another top predator that swims in the same waters as sharks. A swordfish reaches sexual maturity, the age when it can reproduce, when it is five or six years old. Thresher sharks aren't sexually mature until they are nine to thirteen years old. Other late-bloomer sharks can take as long as twenty years to reach sexual maturity. For example, great whites do not mate before they are twenty. They bear very few young, and only some of them survive to adulthood.

SHARK TRUTH

During mating, a male shark holds onto a female by digging his teeth into her skin. So the skin of female sharks is usually much thicker than males' skin.

This is the natural way of keeping apex predator populations in check, because the food chain cannot support too many of them—nor too few. With overfishing, many sharks are caught before they have a chance to reproduce. Others are caught before they have given birth to more than one litter of pups. With fewer pups, the shark population will not stay healthy.

FROM EGGS TO PUPS

All female sharks produce eggs, but sharks vary in the ways the eggs develop into baby sharks. Females mate with males, and they fertilize the eggs through sexual intercourse. With many species of sharks, you can tell males from females by the claspers. Males use these extended pelvic fins (along with their teeth) to hold the females in place while they mate and transfer sperm to eggs for fertilization. All shark eggs are fertilized inside the female's body. What happens after that varies.

Some sharks are oviparous—they lay eggs. The eggs mature and hatch outside the mothers' bodies. Others are viviparous—the eggs are fertilized and develop inside the female's body. The female gives birth to live pups, but she doesn't take care of them after birth. They are on their own.

A female shark can lay from two to eighty eggs, depending on the species. Once the eggs are fertilized, oviparous shark species, such as zebra sharks and necklace carpetsharks, will lay embryo-filled egg sacs—sometimes called mermaid's purses—in shallow coastal ocean waters. There, the embryos live on the yolk in the egg sac until it is gone. Then they emerge from the sac to live in the ocean.

But most female sharks are viviparous. They carry pup embryos (developing sharks) in the uterus. Some unborn sharks, such as smooth hound and

Many sharks, such as this lemon shark (*right*), give live birth. The pup comes out tail first, wrapped in the chorion. This membrane protects the developing shark embryo and helps provide it with nutrients and fluids from the mother prior to birth.

bull sharks, receive their food through a placenta, a tube that carries nutrients from the mother to the embryos. Other embryos (for example, those of makos and cookiecutter sharks) feed by eating unfertilized eggs produced by the mother's ovaries. This is called oophagy. And the sand tiger is a unique species that experiences adelphophagy, which literally means "eating your brother." These embryos feed on one another in

ALONG FOR THE RIDE

Some sharks are solitary. Others travel in a shiver—a school, or group, of sharks. Whale sharks are usually solitary but sometimes travel in groups of other sharks. Some sharks travel in a cluster of smaller, less flashy fish. The smaller fish, known as partner fish, play an important role in the lives of sharks. For example, remoras attach themselves like suction disks to the underside of sharks. Pilot fish swim along with blacktip sharks and oceanic whitetip sharks. By following or attaching themselves to sharks, these

Remoras attach themselves to a lemon shark. Each remora has a specialized dorsal fin covered with a tissue that seals the fish to its shark host.

smaller fish conserve energy they might otherwise spend in swimming or hunting on their own. They feed on the sharks' leftovers and even eat their poop, which is rich in nutrients.

What's in it for the sharks? Pilot fish and remoras pick parasites from their skin, keeping the sharks clean. Parasites suck nutrients from their shark hosts, so by removing parasites, the smaller fish help keep their hosts healthy. Scientists refer to this type of helping relationship between two unrelated species as mutualism, or symbiosis.

the mother's uterus rather than on nutrients that come from a yolk sac or through the placenta. The majority of pups in these litters are eaten before birth.

SEXUAL SUPERPOWERS

From one mating encounter, a female shark can store sperm for later use. Some shark species live alone, and among these species, males and females meet rarely. So solitary females have adapted their reproductive cycle to store a male's sperm for months. The world record for sperm storage by a female shark is a brownbanded bamboo shark (in an aquarium) that stored sperm for three and one-half years! When the female is in the fertile part of her reproductive cycle, the sperm release to fertilize the eggs she produces.

Some female sharks, such as blacktip reef sharks, sawfish, and hammerheads, can even create offspring without mating with a male. During parthenogenesis (from the Greek words *parthenos*, or "virgin," and *genesis*, or "creation"), the mother passes on her female deoxyribonucleic acid (DNA), her genetic information. For example, a blacktip reef shark in the Virginia Aquarium & Marine Science Center produced a pup that was a genetic clone (match) of her own mother. Parthenogenesis can lead to inbreeding, an unhealthy mating practice among related animals that can cause deadly disease and physical weaknesses. But it can be useful for breeding sharks that are endangered and facing extinction.

WHERE THE PUPS ARE

Female shark gestation (pregnancy), on average nine to twelve months, is among the longest of any vertebrate (animals with backbones). Some species have gestation periods up to twenty-four months. Gestation among basking sharks is almost three years. Most sharks have about 20 pups in a litter, although the blue shark lays as many as 135 pups per litter. Once the embryos have matured, the pups are born through the mother's cloaca, or birth canal. Pups look like miniature adults and are able to fend for themselves. Then the relationship with their mothers ends.

LEONIE

Leonie is a female zebra shark at Reef HQ, an aquarium in Townsville, Queensland, Australia. Leonie had spent six years with a male shark mate and produced several litters of pups. In 2012 the aquarium decided to breed fewer sharks and separated the pair. In 2014 Leonie laid eggs anyway, and some of them developed into pups.

As far as scientists know, this is the first time that a female shark has reproduced both sexually and asexually. Leonie first gave birth from eggs her mate had fertilized through mating. She then switched to reproducing *without* her mate directly fertilizing her eggs. Sharks may do this in the wild, but scientists have never actually observed it directly. In fact, researchers rarely are able to observe mating sharks in the ocean.

Christine Dudgeon, a biologist at the University of Queensland, shared her hypothesis about Leonie in an interview with CNN television. She thinks that Leonie may have stored sperm from the last time she had mated with the male shark and used some of that sperm to fertilize the eggs. Or she may have given birth through parthenogenesis, passing only her own genetic material to the pups without the male sperm fertilizing the eggs. Scientists don't exactly know how to explain Leonie's reproduction capacity. "It was definitely a surprise," said Hamish Tristram, a senior aquarist (person who cares for aquarium animals) responsible for caring for the sharks at Reef HQ.

Pupping nurseries along the coasts of the oceans are home to young sharks that may sometimes live in separate groups according to species, size, or gender. The waters are shallow, protected, and filled with the small fry fish that pups eat. Among the US shark nurseries that scientists know about are these:

- Delaware Bay and Chesapeake Bay on the northeastern Atlantic coast of the United States for sandbar sharks;
- Great South Bay off Long Island, New York, for sand tigers;
- Montauk, Long Island, for great whites;
- Bull's Bay, South Carolina, for spinner, dusky, Atlantic sharpnose, and many other sharks;

A female lemon shark swims with her newborn pup. Lemon shark nurseries are typically in tropical, coastal mangrove areas of Bimini, three western islands in the Bahamas. Researchers have found that female lemon sharks often return to the same place where they were born to give birth to their own young years later.

- Dry Tortugas, Florida, for nurse sharks;
- Florida's Atlantic coast for scalloped hammerheads; and
- Louisiana's Gulf of Mexico coast for bull sharks.

How do we know where the nurseries are? Sometimes fleets discover them while fishing. Research is the real key to understanding which areas sharks use and how. Take Delaware Bay. Lying between New Jersey and Delaware, the bay is where the Delaware River widens into an estuary (an area where a river meets and mixes with the sea) before flowing into the Atlantic Ocean. Naeem Willett and Dewayne Fox of Delaware State University, along with Brad Wetherbee of the University of Rhode Island, study sharks. They attach transmitters to the backs or fins of sandbar sharks. The transmitters send signals to the scientists' labs via satellite. The scientists use the data to pinpoint the sharks' locations and to map their movements in those areas. The maps help scientists understand the boundaries of shark habitats and nurseries and can be used to protect sharks.

5
SWIMMING WITH SHARKS

OUR LONG-TERM SATELLITE TRACKING DATA IS SHOWING THAT [INDIVIDUAL SHORTFIN MAKO SHARKS] CAN TRAVEL OVER 10,000 MILES [16,093 KM] IN A SINGLE YEAR, AND THEY ALSO ARE STARTING TO SHOW INDICATIONS OF ROUND-TRIP, REPEATED AND PREDICTABLE MIGRATION PATTERNS.

—MAHMOOD SHIVJI, NOVA SOUTHEASTERN UNIVERSITY'S GUY HARVEY RESEARCH INSTITUTE AND THE SAVE OUR SEAS SHARK RESEARCH CENTER IN FORT LAUDERDALE, FLORIDA

Scuba divers have a universal signal for "there goes a shark": a diver plants the heel of her hand on the top of her head and holds her fingers stiffly upward like a shark's fin. But that's where the similarity between human and shark swimming ends.

A shark masters the water the way a bird masters the air. As the shark swims, its caudal (tail) fin moves side to side, providing the main source of power to propel the shark forward. (Sharks can't swim backward.)

Sharks, such as this blue shark, move through water with a sinusoidal movement of the tail that is S-like, smooth, and repetitive. Sharks have two groups of muscles. Red muscle contracts slowly to provide stamina. It requires a lot of oxygen. White muscle contracts more rapidly for bursts of speed. It does not require as much oxygen.

The motion of the larger upper caudal lobe creates a downward force offset by the lift of the shark's head and chest. The pectoral fins on the sides of the shark's chest are shaped to provide lift. Water flows more slowly over the rounded top edge and faster beneath the straighter bottom edge of the fins. This difference in speed of water flow raises the shark upward and creates thrust. The dorsal (back) fins provide stability by counterbalancing the lift and weight of the front of the shark's body.

Some sharks, such as the porbeagle, have caudal keels—ridges on the sides of their tails between the dorsal fins and caudal fin. The keels make the sharks more hydrodynamic (streamlined) so they can swim faster. Usually sharks swim slowly. The fastest shark may be the shortfin mako. Researchers recorded juvenile shortfin makos moving at 31 to 68 miles (50 to 110 km) per hour. Slower adults may swim in bursts of up to 46 miles (74 km) per hour.

Sharks have techniques for moving through the water to avoid predators and to catch prey. For example, the piked dogfish has a spike in front of

SHARK NOSE

Artists sometime paint sharks on fighter planes. This tradition started in World War II. Aviators boosted their courage and morale—and struck fear into the hearts of their enemies—by painting shark snouts onto the fuselages of the A-10 Warthog. This military plane flies low to the ground to fire the huge built-in cannon protruding from its nose.

each dorsal fin to defend against predators. For hunting, shark tails generally have a short lower lobe so they can press toward the seafloor to find food sources there. Shortfin makos, threshers, spinners, and great whites have what it takes to accelerate through the surface of the water to catch fast-moving prey. Researchers observed a 12-foot (3.5 m) shark that could jump as high as 8 feet (2.4 m) out of the water to pursue a leaping seal. (Check out videos of great whites lunging out of the water after skimming seals. They are not for the faint of heart!)

SHARK SPEED

When you make a beeline for something, you're steering directly for it. When you make a shark line toward a target, the path is S-shaped, more snake than straight shot. This motion—called a sinusoidal (back-and-forth, wavelike) movement—comes from the way muscles that stretch the length of the shark's body move in a repetitive, back-and-forth cycle. First, the muscles contract on the left and then the right, back and forth. The contractions pull the shark's spine one way and then the other. The shark's caudal fin powers this wave of motion, pushing the shark ahead. The fastest sharks start swimming with this wavy motion, then stiffen and straighten to cut down on energy use.

A shark's skin feels like sandpaper under your fingers. You might think a rough surface would create friction and drag, slowing down the shark, but the opposite is true. The denticles on the shark's skin align in a grooved pattern. The water easily flows through rather than around the shark's skin, cutting down on resistance as the shark swims and helping it swim faster.

OLYMPIC SKIN

Swimmers were in an uproar as they prepared for the London Summer Olympics in 2012. At the previous Summer Olympics in Beijing, China, in 2008, many swimmers competed in Speedo LZR suits made from Fastskin FSII. This super-lightweight, thin, high-tech fabric compressed swimmers' bodies into the suit, making them more hydrodynamic and therefore faster in the water. Critics of the fabric felt it gave swimmers who wore it an unfair advantage, so the London Olympics Organizing Committee banned the Fastskin suits. Speedo designers went back to the drawing board. And so did Harvard University biologist George Lauder.

Lauder knew of a "fabric" that was truly the fastest—the mako shark's skin. To test his theory, he created a water treadmill to compare Fastskin to mako sharkskin. The water treadmill pumped water through a tank. Lauder then put two model fish, one made from strips of sharkskin, the other from strips of Fastskin, into the treadmill tank, where water flowed past each one. The result? As Lauder had suspected, the mako-skin fish allowed for faster flow of water than the Fastskin fish. When Lauder sanded the mako-skin fish to remove the denticles, the fish slowed down.

Lauder's next experiment was to build model sharkskin. He used a 3D printer to make denticles from synthetic material. Then he embedded the 3D denticles into a thin, flexible layer of rubberlike material to mimic the sharkskin membrane that holds denticles in place in a real shark. But Lauder's technology fell short. His 3D printer could only print denticles that were ten times the size of a mako's actual denticles, which measure 150 microns, the thickness of a sheet of paper. About his experiment, Lauder said, "The essence of science is being able to control variables and manipulate things in interesting ways. With artificial sharkskin, we can experiment to see what surface structures mean. Maybe we could make a better sharkskin than sharkskin!"

Sharkskin doodle

A HUMANIMAL DOODLE BY KAREN ROMANO YOUNG

(Olympic rings containing text:)
- Olympic Controversy surrounds high-tech...
- Swimsuits, praised AND condemned for increasing
- Speed. They may help swimmers set records
- in London this summer, but
- are they really like the sharkskin that inspired them?

Does this fabric mimic sharkskin?
A close look at Speedo Fastskin® FS II fabric and bonnethead sharkskin

Dr. George V. Lauder and his laboratory team at Harvard University study fish biomechanics and hydrodynamics. They experimented to learn about one of the special fabrics used in the speedy suits many Olympic swimmers swear by. Here's what they did.

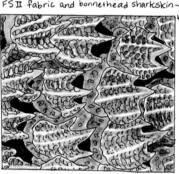

Each sharkskin scale is about 130 microns in diameter—as thick as a sheet of paper or a human hair.

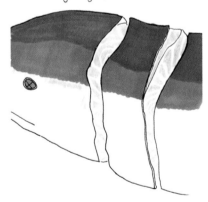

1. Remove shark skin from freshly killed shark. (This is a shortfin mako shark.)

2. Clean muscle and connective tissue from inner surface to make skin strips 1-2 mm thick.

3. Use two strips of skin to make a "sandwich" around a flat-plate foil.

4. Make a matching sandwich using Fastskin fabric.

Water flows this way and is pumped through the tank's system, recirculating.

5. Attach the Sandwich ~ actually a flexible skin membrane ~ to the robotic foil flapping apparatus.

This is Science in Action!

Dr. Lauder

When you flap the foil back and forth, it starts to **swim** forward. It's like a swimming treadmill. On a _walking_ treadmill, if you walk fast you might turn up the treadmill speed so you don't crash into the front of the machine. If you slow down, you turn the treadmill down so you don't fall off the back. So the treadmill has to be moving at the same speed you're walking at, in order for you to walk in place. This **swimming** treadmill is the same. It gives us the speed at which the foil — or robotic fish — moves.

So, **which** Skin-Sandwich robotic-flapping Lauder Lab fish **won the race?**

Based on **skin**, it's a **win** for the **shortfin**.

The Lauder Lab team didn't just compare the Shark and the Suit. To see if the skin made the difference, they "sanded" off the sharkskin's dentricles, those tooth-like scales, and turned the Fastskin inside-out.

➤ the SHARK slowed down, BUT the Suit's speed did not change.

Lauder's conclusion? The Suit's speed is due to factors other than the fabric. Some <u>possibilities</u>:

? Suit tightness helps the swimmer maintain **form** (posture and motion) when tired.

? Construction of suit cuts drag.

? Suit tightness improves the swimmer's circulation, increasing oxygen intake.

May the best swimmer win!

Important Question: **How** do **sharks** swim so fast? _Important Answer:_ **Sharkskin** dentricles improve the flow of water over the shark's body, ↓ decreasing ↓ drag and ↑ increasing ↑ thrust as the skin **bends**. But there's more to the answer: Lauder says the effect of sharkskin is **LOST** if it's not moving. But <u>live</u> sharks move _continually_. The skin bending is the **key**.

VACATION MIGRATION

But why do sharks swim? And where are they going? Sharks migrate mostly to breed and feed. Spiny dogfish, for example, migrate many miles to pursue their prey around the ocean. One tagged individual swam from Washington State to Japan—a 5,000-mile (8,047 km) one-way journey. Salmon sharks swim from the coast of Alaska to subtropical parts of the Pacific Ocean near Hawaii. One salmon shark traveled 11,321 miles (18,219 km) over 640 days—almost half the distance around Earth. Great white sharks wintering off San Francisco, California, also migrate seasonally 2,280 miles (3,669 km) to waters near the Hawaiian Islands. Many stop off at a feeding area halfway between Hawaii and Baja California Peninsula, Mexico, that is so popular with migrating sharks that scientists call it the Shark Cafe.

SHARK TRUTH

Leather makers sometimes use sharkskin to make leather fabrics. Sharkskin leather that still has the denticles is called shagreen. It is perfect for nonskid material.

Some sharks follow predictable routes—just as people do when they flock to the same beach at certain times every year. For example, researchers in a small plane flying over the Atlantic Ocean see and take photographs every year of the annual blacktip shark migration off the coast of eastern Florida. Every winter this shark migration, the nation's largest, creates headline news in Florida. Anyone who looks at the pictures of the sharks is bound to ask, "What are all those sharks doing at the beach?"

According to Florida Atlantic University shark researchers, about eleven thousand to fourteen thousand blacktips swarm this part of coastal Florida every February. From their plane, the researchers try to count every one. In the winter, the sharks are swimming southward from cold northern waters to warmer waters, following prey. In summer they'll swim back north again, following the same types of prey animals.

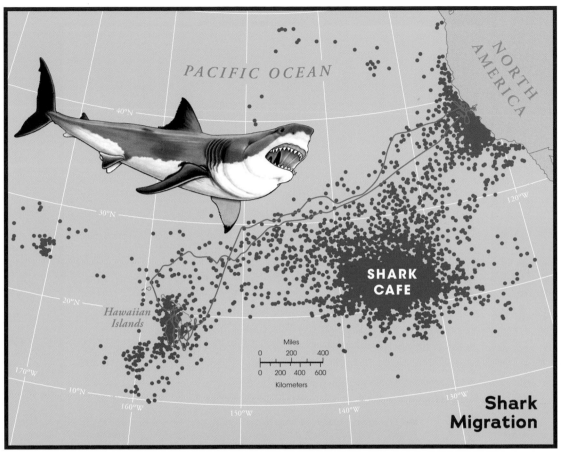

This infographic shows the annual spring migration territory of the great white shark. The Shark Cafe is a spot about halfway between western Mexico and Hawaii where the sharks stay from April to July. Scientists aren't quite sure if they go there for mating or for food. In winter the sharks feed and mate along the coasts of central and Southern California.

Not all sharks migrate. Nurse sharks and bonnethead sharks are among the homebodies. Of the shark species that do migrate, coastal pelagic sharks such as blacktip, tiger, and sandbar sharks may swim about 1,000 miles (1,600 km) a year. They follow food, sticking with whatever water temperature is hospitable to their prey. Highly pelagic sharks sprint across the ocean. Among them are the fastest swimmers, such as blue and mako sharks.

THE SHARK WORLD'S HUCKLEBERRY FINN

Bull sharks (*below*) usually live in shallow coastal waters. But some of them don't seem to care whether they are in salt water or freshwater. They will swim from the salty Gulf of Mexico right up the freshwaters of the Mississippi River, where Mark Twain's fictional character Huckleberry Finn took his famous river journey. Bull sharks have even swum up the river as far north as Illinois. Other bull sharks live in the Amazon River 2,500 miles (4,023 km) from the Atlantic coast of Brazil in South America. Others seem to live in the Ganges River in India or in Lake Nicaragua, a freshwater lake in Central America.

Scientists aren't sure *why* bull sharks inhabit freshwater, but they have figured out *how* they tolerate it. Sharks need a particular level of salt in their bodies to survive. So when they are in freshwater, glands near their tails recycle the salt already in their bodies so they don't lose any of it as they swim in bodies of freshwater. But what's the use of leaving the big salty ocean in the first place? Mike Heithaus, who studies sharks at Florida International University, told *National Geographic* that "probably the biggest reason is that [freshwater tolerance] allows the juveniles, the little guys, to be in a place that's relatively safe from being eaten by other sharks."

They ride currents to make better time as they cover great distances for food and reproduction. For example, researchers have tracked female blue sharks that mate in the spring and early summer off the coast of New England and swim across the Atlantic Ocean to pup off the western coast of Africa. They make their return trip up to fourteen months later by way of the North Equatorial Current, which moves westward across the Atlantic Ocean and toward the Caribbean Sea. From there the sharks catch the Gulf Stream current to move back up the eastern coast of the United States to their mating grounds. All told, the round-trip is 9,500 miles (15,289 km).

Sharks also migrate vertically, diving as deep as 2,900 feet (884 m) to live in colder waters during the winter. They slow down in these waters and need less food, so they eat less in winter. In summer, as the waters warm, the sharks return to the surface to feed on abundant food supplies there.

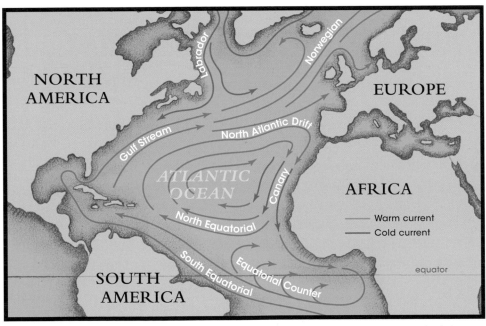

Sharks follow natural ocean currents and temperatures in their annual migratory treks. This infographic shows major currents in the Atlantic Ocean.

Tiger sharks will travel long distances to find food. And they are not picky eaters. Researchers sometimes call them garbage cans of the sea because they literally eat trash that humans toss or leave behind—everything from boat cushions to bags of potatoes.

HOW SHARKS FIND THEIR WAY

Scientists can't pin down whether sharks navigate with their noses or with a sense of their position on Earth's electromagnetic field. The answer is likely a combination of factors. Earth is surrounded by an invisible skin of electromagnetic charge that emerges from one pole, sheaths the planet, and enters again through the other pole. Every spot on Earth has a different and precise electromagnetic charge. Many animals instinctively sense the charge and use it to determine where they are in space and to orient themselves toward a target or destination.

Certain sharks instinctively swim along paths with waypoints along Earth's electromagnetic field. Tiger sharks are one species that seem to have a mental map of the ocean in their heads. They migrate enormous distances (sometimes thousands of miles). Within smaller areas, they swim in straight lines—what scientists call directed walks—toward food sources. Scientists who observe the sharks say the animals seem to target the sources and know how to get there without wavering in their course.

Older tiger sharks swim along straighter paths than younger ones do. This indicates to scientists that tiger sharks learn their way around, remembering destinations and previous routes. How are they doing it? Scientists aren't precisely sure. Other wayfinding animals such as sea turtles, trout, and yellowfin tuna have magnetite crystals in their heads. The crystals respond to Earth's electromagnetic signals, providing these animals with a natural Global Positioning System (GPS). But sharks don't have magnetite, so how are they finding their way? One clue comes from *when* they are finding their way. Yannis Papastamatiou of the Florida Museum of Natural History led a study to learn more about how sharks orient themselves. In an interview about the study, he told the British Broadcasting Corporation that "the sharks' ability to navigate is open to debate, but the fact that many of these [shark] journeys took place at night—you and I would think there's nothing to orientate to, so orientating to magnetic fields is one possibility."

Scientists do know that sharks rely on their ampullae of Lorenzini for navigation. These jelly-filled pores in their snouts respond to electrical signals. As sharks swim through Earth's electromagnetic field, scientists say, their bodies generate current that the ampullae pick up. Magnetoreception—receiving the charges—is the key to the sharks' mental map and helps them adjust their paths when they need to.

The Papastamatiou study also looked at other shark species to see if they too swim in straight lines. Threshers were a yes, but blacktip reef sharks were a no. Their walks were random, not direct. Scientists know that blacktips have a smaller range, staying near reefs. So they think their navigation system may not require as many sensory factors as sharks that move across much bigger territories.

FOLLOWING THEIR NOSES?

Andrew Nosal is a researcher at the Scripps Institution of Oceanography and Birch Aquarium, in La Jolla, California. For one study, Nosal caught, tagged, and transported twenty-six leopard sharks 6 miles (10 km) from

Leopard sharks have a distinctive pattern of leopardlike brown or black spots on their bodies. They are sometimes known as cat sharks. Researchers aren't sure how they navigate.

their coastal home to an area much farther out to sea. To learn more about how they would navigate their way back home, Nosal stuffed the nasal passages of eleven of the leopard sharks with cotton to weaken their sense of smell. He left fifteen other sharks with fully functional noses. The discovery? The fifteen sharks sniffed out their location immediately, pulled a U-turn, and headed back home. No problem. The eleven sharks with plugged noses had a more difficult time of it. They lost their sense of direction at first and moved randomly and slowly. All the same, they eventually turned toward shore and made their way back home.

As with much science, seeing what happens is sometimes easier than interpreting why it happens. Nosal figured that each of the twenty-six sharks was eventually able to sniff out chemicals in the ocean that they recognized as smelling like home. The closer the sharks were to shore, the denser the chemical scent and the more confident the animals were about their location. Other scientists who heard about the study disagreed. They pointed out that even the sharks with plugged noses turned toward the coast, so other factors for navigation might be at play. One scientist suggested that the sharks showed random movement because they simply didn't like having something stuffed into their noses.

Another team of researchers, trying to figure out how blacktip reef sharks find their way without magnetoreception, did a similar experiment with young blacktips. Jayne Gardiner and a team from the New College of Florida in Tampa worked with five blacktips. The team plugged the sharks' noses and found they got lost. "We have bits and pieces [about navigation] from various animals, but we don't have the whole story yet," Gardiner told the multimedia science website *Seeker*. "Most of us are in agreement that it's a fairly similar story across different animals."

6
WHAT DO **SHARK RESEARCHERS** DO AT **SEA?**

A SUCCESSFUL DIVE IS USUALLY A DIVE WHERE YOU ARE FORTUNATE TO SEE SHARKS OF ANY SORT!

—SYLVIA EARLE, MARINE BIOLOGIST AND OCEANOGRAPHER, TWITTER FEED, MAY 2017

In an office at National Geographic headquarters in Washington, DC, South African marine biologist Alison Kock taught a visitor how to tag a mock great white shark. She used a long pole with a steel loop on one end. A handle on the other end was for pulling to snap the loop tight over the shark's massive upright fin. The visitor leaned over the rail (a desk), across the churning ocean (the office floor), and toward

Oceanic whitetip sharks have noticeable whitish-tipped fins. They live in warm tropical waters all over the world. This whitetip is swimming with pilot fish in the Red Sea, which lies between northeastern Africa and Saudi Arabia. The pilot fish clean parasites from the shark, while the shark protects the fish from predators.

the approaching fin (a wooden triangle on a stand on a table) to try to snag it with the loop and snap it tight. The visitor missed the first six times. Imagine how difficult it is to tag a shark in the ocean!

Scientists studying sharks use tags as a primary technology in their work. When Mahmood Shivji plays tag with sharks, he expects to deal with sea chop, boat pitch, and—oh yeah—a big, aggressive, toothy shark. Shivji, director of the Guy Harvey Research Institute at Nova Southeastern University in Fort Lauderdale, Florida, has tagged hundreds of big sharks to follow them and learn more about their migrations. Since scientists first began tagging sharks in the 1920s, researchers have learned vast amounts about where sharks go, what they do there, and why. From tagging, we know, for example, that mako sharks swim the farthest of any shark and that blue sharks maintain the highest speed over their migrations. Makos are faster in short bursts. We know that sand tiger sharks swim along the seafloor, while oceanic whitetips stick to the surface waters. We know that female lemon sharks give birth to their pups in the same waters—off Bimini, in the Bahamas—where they were born.

To tag sharks, most scientists catch them with rod and reel. They sometimes chum the water first to attract them with bloody bait. When the animals approach the bait, the researchers use a sharp tool that resembles a dart to shoot a transponder (radio receiver) tag into the shark's flesh. The tag will ping the shark's location, information about its physical condition, and data such as depth and temperature of the water. The pings "talk" to acoustic buoys in the sea or transmit data to satellites in space. From there, the signals go to scientists in labs on ships or on land.

OCEARCH

Then came *Ocearch*, a 126-foot (38 m) boat captained by expedition leader Chris Fischer, founder of the organization Ocearch. Aboard *Ocearch*, tagging goes like this. The crew pushes half-frozen mackerel through a tube into the sea to chum the water. When a shark nears the tube, the team snags it on a line and brings it atop the underwater platform. A hydraulic lift elevates the platform and its catch from beneath the surface of the water to the deck of the boat.

During a fifteen-minute countdown, researchers take blood samples, parasite samples, and photographs of the shark. They also tag the shark through a well-coordinated team effort. The crew covers the shark's eyes with a damp towel to keep them lubricated. The team also pumps ocean water through the animal's mouth and gills to keep it hydrated and oxygenated. Then they release the tagged shark.

Ocearch's Global Shark Tracker smartphone app and website allow users to follow sharks in real time. The website gets millions of hits. Shark Tracker has a popular fan club on Facebook, and many of the sharks have their own Twitter accounts. Popular sharks include great whites Curly, CubsWin, and Genie (named for ichthyologist Eugenie Clark).

Collaborating scientist Robert Hueter of Marine Mote Laboratory in Florida says that complete data on big sharks was difficult to get before Ocearch came along. With easy tagging and sampling, Ocearch is providing information that is changing research dramatically. Like Hueter, marine biologist Gregory Skomal of the Massachusetts Division of Marine Fisheries was an early Ocearch collaborator. He was eager to use this valuable new method to learn more about great whites. "We've learned that what we previously thought about this species isn't exactly true," he told *CBS This Morning* in 2012. "They're doing things we never thought they were capable of. . . . I never expected a great white shark to be off the coast of New England in February, that they could survive in those [cold] temperatures," Skomal said.

By 2016 Skomal had tagged one hundred great white sharks. *The Boston Globe* called it a testament to the surging population of the sharks off Cape Cod. That year Skomal told *Scientific American* that the work of Ocearch, which tags sharks in federal waters, was coming too close to his own tagging work in Massachusetts waters, just half a mile (0.8 km) away. One problem was bait. Ocearch's practice of luring sharks by chumming the waters had the potential, Skomal said, to disrupt sharks' normal behavior—the normal behavior he was trying to document through a five-year study. Skomal was also noticing that being hauled out of the water and put aboard *Ocearch* seemed to deter sharks from returning to that area.

DISRUPTING SHARK BEHAVIOR?

In 2012 and 2013, Skomal and Fischer, Ocearch's founder, had worked together on shark tagging, using *Ocearch* to tag several sharks. One was Mary Lee, named for Fischer's mother, and one of the sharks made most popular by Global Shark Tracker. The 16-foot (4.9 m), 3,456-pound (1,568 kg) shark has traveled more than 25,000 miles (40,233 km) since her tagging. But she has never returned to the waters where she was tagged. The experience may have changed her natural swimming patterns. Skomal said that 80 percent of the sharks he had tagged with acoustic tags, which don't require pulling the sharks out of the water, returned to the areas where they had been tagged.

So Skomal asked Ocearch to stop tagging great whites off the coast of Massachusetts until his five-year study wrapped up in 2018. That way he could be sure that the behaviors he observed—and the population numbers he estimated—were correct. Skomal worries that chumming disrupts sharks' natural hunting habits—the behavior he prefers to document. But the Ocearch folks said they have no evidence that their work is disruptive to sharks. They continued tagging—

SHARK TRUTH

Mary Lee, a great white shark, has more than 125,000 followers on Twitter! Check her out at @MaryLeeShark.

and through their work and the accompanying app, they are bringing attention to the far-ranging swimming patterns of sharks of several species. The work of both researchers has great value to human understanding of sharks. But what should happen when research projects overlap?

AN EYE ON SHARKS

Tagging helps researchers learn about sharks where humans have easy access. The next step for science is to determine sharks' activities where humans can't so easily follow them. How? With cameras. Strapped onto shark fins, attached to their backs with suction cups, and carried by robots, cameras— well, they tag along.

Cameras first got into the world of sharks with Crittercam. These small cameras were the predecessors of GoPros, action cameras that can take still photos as well as video footage on land and underwater. Crittercams can be attached temporarily to an animal's back or head. Crittercam inventor Greg Marshall recalled what he saw one day in 1986 when he was a graduate student in marine science diving off the coast of Belize, a country in Central America. He spotted a shark with a remora attached to its belly. Up to then, the only film of underwater sharks also featured human divers near the animals and, therefore, sharks responding to them. "I wanted to disassociate shark behavior with that response to people," Marshall said. So he began developing Crittercams to aid scientific observation of animals without humans nearby. "We have seen surprising things once we took ourselves out of the equation," Marshall said. "For the length of time that the cameras are attached, they record (and sometimes transmit) images that show what sharks are doing, so that researchers can match their activity with the data showing where they go as well as their speed, heart rate, and other vital signs. The result is a more complete story of a shark's life," observes Marshall.

Maybe you've seen those videos of seals leaping from the water just ahead of the hungry jaws of a hunting great white? Footage taken when Alison Kock used her tagging mojo to put a Crittercam on a great white shark off Seal Island, South Africa, filled in the blanks of what was going on underwater, providing a shark's-eye view of the elusive hunt. It's the stuff of nightmares, if you're afraid of sharks—or if you're a seal.

Skomal also relies on Crittercams to study sharks. In 2007 he published the results of studies he did using Crittercams on six grey reef sharks in the central Pacific Ocean. Skomal wanted to learn more about how sharks fare after recreational and commercial fishers throw them back into the water. Skomal and his colleagues hooked six grey reef sharks and tagged them with the cameras. From the footage, they determined that after release, only one of the six sharks seemed to have a bumpy recovery from its time on the hook and out of the water. He thinks that for the most part, catch and release doesn't have a dramatic impact on shark behavior. However, the longer interaction of the Ocearch routine may alter shark behavior.

WHAT MAKES A GOOD FISH GO BAD?

Skomal's colleague Phillip Lobel, of Boston University, piggybacked on Skomal's research. He placed Crittercams on six grey reef sharks, put on his own scuba gear, and dived with the sharks off the coast of Palau. He wasn't alone. Scuba-diving tourists love the coral reefs off the coast of this island nation in the western Pacific Ocean. Here they are likely to see grey reef sharks, bull sharks, and rays. To assure that tourists will see a lot of sharks on their dives, tour operators will sometimes dangle chum in the water by hand to lure the animals closer. Lobel wanted to know whether chumming impacts normal shark behavior and the ecosystem of the reef. He also wanted to judge whether chumming adds risk for scuba divers. He noticed that "there [was] always concern by the dive guides when unfamiliar sharks came into a hand-feeding area." They worried that sharks that broke their normal habits could behave in other unpredictable ways, endangering divers.

But what happens when an invading species (in this case, humans) arrives in an environment where sharks live? Does shark behavior change? Lobel wanted to know. He went to Blue Corner, a dive site in Palau and the world's first shark preserve, established in 2009. He also went to a marine preserve in another South Pacific island nation, Fiji. As Lobel observed grey reef sharks in their natural habitats, he looked for factors that might, as he put it, "make a good fish go bad." He realized that sharks from parts of the ocean far away from both islands that weren't accustomed to seeing scuba divers would sometimes act more aggressively than local sharks that were used to divers. And his team noticed that areas where grey reef sharks acted aggressively were polluted with mercury and lead. The scientists think that these and other pollutants may impact shark behavior. Icthyologists have more work to do to determine exactly which factors contribute to unusual shark behaviors.

To learn more about shark behavior near humans, Carl Meyer and Kim Holland of the Hawai'i Institute of Marine Biology looked at sharks attracted to diving cages off the island of Oahu. Diving cages are a popular way for tourists to see sharks. Tourists put on diving gear and descend into chummed waters in shark-proof diving cages for a close-up shark encounter. Scientists sometimes observe sharks this way too. Meyer and Holland caught thirty-six Galapagos and sandbar sharks at cage-diving sites and implanted them with small ultrasonic tags to track them. They wanted to find out whether the sharks were following the tour boats back toward shore—and possibly threatening swimmers there. The verdict? Not guilty. The sharks swam to nearby islands, but none followed the tourist boats or approached people on the beach.

A tourist in a diving cage off Mexico's Pacific coast photographs a great white shark. Researchers are learning more about if and how human presence in shark territory impacts the animals' behavior.

Tagging helps divers, both tourists and researchers, get a good look at sharks. When they are knowledgeable, citizen scientists can identify an animal's biological sex and figure out which sharks are sexually active. They can spot male claspers, and females may show bite scars from mating or may be visibly pregnant. Scientists will place a small acoustic bracelet tag to sharks' caudal peduncle (tail). Like other acoustic tags, these tags record baseline information about the normal travels of pregnant and mating sharks. The tags also record how shark bodies respond to their activities, such as how their breathing rate changes as they move. Establishing a baseline of data for an animal is vital to understanding an animal's health and well-being over time and in different conditions.

As divers swim and dive with sharks—or turtles or whales or dolphins or other charismatic megafauna (big animal superstars)—they see firsthand the majesty of the animals. They also observe how the animals live within their environments and how they adjust to or suffer from changes to their habitat. That's valuable. As Greg Skomal says, "With education comes respect, and with respect comes conservation and preservation."

TAG GUIDE

Shark scientists use a variety of tags to attach to sharks and then track them to learn more about their behaviors and movements in their ocean habitats.

ID TAGS

Spaghetti, business card, or anchor tags are ID tags with a dart to anchor them through the skin and into the shark's muscle. The shark is caught, tagged, and released. The tag usually bears the date of tagging and a request to report the shark to the agency or researcher that tagged it. This way, the next person who sees the shark can contribute to charting the animal's path through the sea.

TRANSMITTING TAGS

Acoustic tags, or pingers, are attached with a harpoon from a small boat. This method is less disruptive than catch-and-release tagging. Acoustic tags ping, or send an acoustic signal, to communicate with underwater buoys when the shark nears them. The tag sends data from the shark to the buoy. Then the buoy uploads information to the researcher's computer.

Acoustic bracelets are metal tags that fit over the shark's caudal peduncle. Research divers attach it to the shark's tail, and it works just like an acoustic tag.

Smart Position or Temperature Transmitting (SPOT) tags communicate data to satellites in real time when the tagged shark fin breaks the sea surface. Research teams capture the shark to attach the tag to its dorsal fin.

Pop-Off Satellite Archival Tags (PSATs) are programmed to detach from the shark after a set time. They upload their data via satellite.

CAMERAS

Animal-borne imaging cameras attach to an animal's back with a suction cup or to the fin with a metal band. Crittercam is one type of animal-born imaging camera. Teams attach the cameras to the shark at the surface. The cameras capture film as the animal dives.

UP AND COMING

Scientists who watch sharks in the wild are developing creative technologies to help them in their work. For example, for safety and for the most useful observations of sharks, researchers must keep their distance from the animals while also collecting reliable data. Mikki McComb-Kobza is the director of the Ocean First Institute in Boulder, Colorado. She worked with teens at Skyline High School in nearby Longmont to develop an instrument for measuring whale sharks and great whites from a distance.

Students in the school's aquatic robotics club had worked with the Denver Zoo to design a twin-laser photogrammetry device for measuring frogs. The device combines a GoPro camera and two lasers. McComb-Kobza asked the students to create a version of the design for her shark research. She wanted a device for measuring the length of a shark's body without having to get into the water with it. Her target? A female great white spotted shark in the Pacific Ocean off Baja California, Mexico—the biggest of its kind ever seen.

"What we built is cheap, easy to use and easy to put together," explained student Marco Guerrero. The lasers shine two points of light onto the shark as the camera snaps its picture. The laser lights show up in the photo as points. Because researchers know the distance between the laser points, they can measure the length of the shark's body at a distance.

McComb-Kobza said, "Being able to take students on expeditions and having them measure sharks underwater with their tools and then surfacing and yelling out how excited they are, 'Do you see that Mikki?, Can you believe that?' That is another really unbelievable experience because it's deeply impactful, and for me, there's no other thing as important as knowing that you've impacted somebody and opened their eyes to something they didn't know before."

Like McComb-Kobza, biologist Greg Skomal travels the world studying sharks, and he relies on sophisticated technologies to do his work. In 2010 Skomal began to study basking sharks. As with his research on great whites, he uses satellite transponder tags. He also relies on robotic autonomous

HARRY LINDO AND HELL'S BAY

Harry Lindo is a male tiger shark. Mahmood Shivji and his team at the Guy Harvey Research Institute tagged Harry in 2009 as part of the Bermuda Shark Project. Harry holds a shark record—he's the shark that tracked the longest distance before losing his tag—27,000 miles (43,452 km) in fifteen months. During that time, he cycled between Bermuda and the Caribbean islands of Barbuda and Antigua. Researchers are following other sharks that seem to be competing to break Harry's record!

In 2017 a male mako shark named Hell's Bay set a different record—the longest time tracked by tag: six hundred days, just a little more than a year and a half, after it was tagged off Ocean City, Maryland. During that time, Hell's Bay traveled 13,000 miles (20,921 km). Shivji said, "Having Hell's Bay report for as long as he has is fantastic because we're able to really get a detailed look at mako migration behavior over a good amount of time. He was like the Energizer Bunny—he kept going and going and going, and luckily did not get captured like many of our other sharks."

underwater vehicles (AUVs) to follow the sharks in the water. The vehicles record and relay data back to computers on the research vessel.

Basking sharks get their name from their habit of swimming at the surface of the water in the sunshine during warm weather, as if working on their tans. But where do basking sharks go in winter? Do they go deeper in the ocean for the winter months? Do they go far? Skomal wanted to know.

So he and his team tagged basking sharks—the world's second-largest fish (after whale sharks). With the data from the satellites, Skomal and his team followed the sharks through their surface migrations from New England waters across the tropics, an area on either side of the equator, all the way to the Atlantic coast of Brazil. This is a trip of thousands of miles, including lots of zigzags and dives. The satellite data also allowed Skomal to follow the sharks to depths where few researchers expected they would go, at times staying there for months. These were the first set of results to show any fish species crossing the equator during its migration. However, Skomal and his team couldn't determine the sex of the basking sharks they were following. So they couldn't match up migration patterns with sex to figure out which sharks were going where and for what purpose.

A BIRD'S-EYE VIEW OF SHARKS

Marine biologist Chris Lowe is the director of the Shark Lab at California State University, Long Beach. The Shark Lab is older than Lowe. Biologist Donald R. Nelson founded the lab in 1966. He was one of the first to tag sharks with acoustic tags to transmit information about them from sea to shore. Lowe's family has a history as whalers and fishers. While Lowe was pursuing a degree in zoology at the University of Hawaii, he got interested in hammerhead sharks. He has made his career out of understanding the movement, physiology, and behavior of these sharks.

In the twenty-first century, the Shark Lab still uses acoustic tags as well as newer-technology satellite tags to study sharks. Lowe and his team also use an autonomous (self-flying) hexacopter equipped with audio and video. This helicopter-like drone has six individual rotors. Lowe and his team can program it to fly transects, fixed paths over a specific area of the ocean, to take video footage for counting and measuring sharks in the water below. The team also has the option of operating the hexacopter by radio control. The hexacopter can provide accurate data, even if the sharks are well underwater or the hexacopter is high up.

In the past, researchers have had to rely on statistics from fisheries, counts by divers in the ocean, and underwater cameras loaded with bait to determine the number of sharks in various parts of the ocean. All of these methods are intrusive to sharks, and scientists worry that they don't provide a completely accurate view of natural shark behavior. They hope that drones and other autonomous technologies will help them observe sharks acting naturally—doing what they do when no human is near. For example, in early 2017, Jeremy Kiszka and a team from Florida International University reported on their study of sharks along a shallow reef in Mo'orea, an island in the South Pacific Ocean. They flew a drone 40 feet (12 m) above the sea surface. The drone caught images that showed that areas with provisioning (bait fish that dive groups plant to attract sharks for tourists) draw higher numbers of sharks than would otherwise be expected in those areas of the ocean. These results confirm Lobel's finding that provisioning for tourists changes the natural behavior of sharks by luring them to areas outside their usual territory. To learn even more about how sharks use their environments, Kiszka hopes to use cameras mounted *on* sharks next.

SEND IN THE ROBOT

Here comes REMUS SharkCam—it's torpedo-shaped, it's a high-visibility yellow, and it's pursuing a shark in a deep dive. REMUS, a type of AUV, stands for Remote Environmental Monitoring Units. It is a swimming robotic underwater glider that can locate, track, and film tagged sharks at sea. Its software pings on tagged sharks and navigates the glider toward a target. When it nears the shark, it slows and stands off at a distance so that it doesn't seem threatening to the shark. At that distance, REMUS's six cameras can film the shark going about its business without interference from people in the water. (The sharks do sometimes treat REMUS itself as an intruder.) While REMUS is filming, it is also sending data to shore-based scientists who can change orders on the fly. For example, they can adapt the glider's depth or speed. If you go to the SharkCam website at http://www.whoi.edu/osl/sharkcam, you can see video of a curious shark approaching the glider to see what's up—and the glider camera getting a close-up of the shark. Sharks studied so far with REMUS technology include great whites and basking sharks off Cape Cod. The technology can be adapted to study other seagoing animals, including sea turtles.

Marine biologist Greg Skomal and engineer Roger Stokey of Woods Hole Oceanographic Institution (WHOI) have deployed SharkCam in great white shark habitats including Guadalupe Island, on Mexico's western coast, and the waters off Cape Cod. In both spots, SharkCam film revealed the sharks' approach to stalking and killing seals—and in attacking the SharkCam. Even if you know it's coming, when a shark snatches the SharkCam, it's a shock.

Sharks that take the SharkCam as bait have done damage to the cameras. Scientists want to see the animals acting as they normally would in the wild, not responding to an invader robot camera. So the institution's ocean vehicle systems engineer Amy Kukulya said, "We need to make this thing more stealth and under-the-radar for sharks, not something they're interested in attacking."

For now, SharkCam scientists treasure the stories the films help them tell. For example, when they sent a glider into shark-filled waters at night in 2013, they spied a strong current of water pulling a motionless great white shark straight into its powerful flow. (Strong currents will carry along even big boats resting at anchor.) It was the first time anyone had ever observed a great white shark sleeping.

A team from the Woods Hole Oceanographic Institution took a REMUS SharkCam to Guadalupe Island, Mexico. WHOI caught footage of this great white shark attacking the underwater robot.

7
WHAT DO **SHARK RESEARCHERS** DO **ONSHORE?**

THE INITIAL REACTION OF KIDS, FACES UPTURNED
AND EYES WIDE OPEN, GAZING AT THE SHARK TANK,
MOST OFTEN CONVEYS A COMBINATION OF ELEVATED
ENERGY, BRAVADO, AND ANXIETY. . . . IN THE QUIET OF
NIGHT AND TRUST OF CLOSING EYES TO SLEEP, AND
THEN AWAKENING TO FIND THAT ALL IS WELL, THE KIDS'
DEMEANOR AND ATTITUDES ARE OFTEN TRANSFORMED
INTO CALM, AWE, AND RESPECT.

—CLARINDA HIGGINS, FORMER ASSISTANT CURATOR OF EDUCATION, THE
MARITIME AQUARIUM IN NORWALK, CONNECTICUT

The Monterey Bay Aquarium in central California is the second-largest aquarium in the world and hosts about two million visitors each year. The aquarium's shark tank includes sevengill, leopard, spiny dogfish, and Pacific angel sharks. The shark tank is 90 feet (27 m) long and has an hourglass shape so the sharks have room to turn and glide.

In sweatpants or pajamas, they nestle into cozy sleeping bags on benches padded with carpeting, in the company of their best friends. Overheard: whispers between kids, adult voices nearby, and a few snores. When they turn over and peek at their surroundings, they see rippling light and swimming forms. These are undulating fish, flapping rays, and the smooth, slow S-swim of sharks. *In the room where these kids are sleeping?*

The Maritime Aquarium in Norwalk, Connecticut, hosts sleep-ins in the big visitor area outside the massive glass windows of the sand tiger shark tank. Does anyone get a good night's sleep in a slumber party with the shadowy forms and glass-eyed grins of sharks? One thing's for sure. The kids get a fabulous opportunity to watch the animals.

Many shark species are difficult to keep in captivity. They need big tanks and lots of salt water. They sometimes become disoriented and depressed, stop eating, and die. In the wild, whale sharks swim about 33 feet (10 m) deep, covering distances of up to 21 miles (34 km) a day. In captivity, they can't maintain this same depth and distance, so they swim in circles—hundreds of circles a day.

In the wild, whale sharks can live to be a century old. In captivity, the life span is far less. From 1980 to 1998, Japan's Okinawa Churaumi Aquarium kept a total of sixteen sharks. They lived an average of only 502 days (a little more than a year) in captivity.

Sharks, especially large or pelagic sharks, rarely are kept in aquariums for a long time. Sharks in captivity are, however, much easier to study to learn about their swimming, sensory abilities, and sometimes reproduction. But not all scientists agree that studying sharks in captivity is the best way to understand their natural behaviors and life cycle.

And yet, sharks in aquariums do inspire young people to become scientists. Pioneering shark scientist Eugenie Clark fell in love with sharks as a child, gazing through the glass of the shark tank at the New York Aquarium. These days she might be the first to sign up for a sleepover with sharks!

JAWS IN THE HOUSE

As any research diver can tell you, capturing a shark and bringing it back to shore alive is not easy. Aquarists at aquariums will also tell you that it's not easy to keep sharks in captivity. So why do we keep sharks in aquariums? And what are the benefits of having them there?

It's true that living in captivity shortens a shark's life span. But aquariums can successfully keep sharks for years. Researchers have learned more about shark physiology, including how female sharks reproduce without males. And aquariums raise money to pay for important shark research.

Among the biggest success stories is the sandbar shark. Its habitat is close to shore in many locations that have aquariums, so the shark doesn't have to be transported far once it is caught. Some sharks, such as whitetip

TONIC IMMOBILITY

Knowledgeable shark handlers—fishers, researchers, and aquarists—have a seemingly magic trick for subduing sharks. They take advantage of tonic immobility, an instinctive shark reflex that is shared by other animals, including chickens, opossums, and trout. By gently turning certain sharks—such as great whites and tiger sharks—onto their backs, the reflex kicks in. The sharks' muscles slow down their reaction time, and the animals become temporarily paralyzed, as if playing dead—a strategy called thanatosis. (*Thanatos* is the Greek word for "death.")

In the wild, some whales know how to trigger the reflex in sharks. The whale will grab a shark in its jaws, turn it over, and hold it in position. Totally still, the shark does not thrash its tail or gnash its teeth. Then the whale can eat the shark easily and quickly.

How does tonic immobility work? Scientists think that being on its back is a disorienting position for a shark. It overwhelms the animal's senses and puts it into a relaxed trance that resembles hypnosis—or death. After about fifteen minutes, the shark will suddenly snap out of its trance and go into action again. "We've never seen a shark look so adorable," said one filmmaker.

reef sharks, will hunt other fish in their tanks. But as long as aquarium divers feed them enough food, sandbar sharks won't get hungry and become aggressive and competitive.

A FISH OUT OF THE OCEAN

Before 1981 the longest any great white shark had ever been held in captivity was one day. That year SeaWorld entertainment marine park in San Diego kept a young great white for sixteen days before aquarists became concerned about its health. When the shark began having convulsions and problems with swimming, they thought it best to release it to the wild. The animal was caught by a fisher only days later.

From 2004 to 2013, Monterey Bay Aquarium in California was the only public aquarium in the world to display great white sharks. The aquarium had six of them, one after another—in the massive 1.2 million-gallon (4.5 million L) Open Sea exhibit. The first, a female, stayed 198 days before she attacked two smaller sharks in the exhibit. After that, aquarists released her back to sea. None of the others stayed very long. One major problem: they wouldn't eat. None of the sharks died in captivity, but aquarists decided to let them go before they got too thin and weak. In 2013 the aquarium announced it would quit trying to keep great whites in captivity. It wasn't a great life for the sharks, and visitors don't seem to care if the aquarium has great white sharks or not. They love the aquarium no matter what.

Great whites fail in captivity. They become depressed or disoriented to the point of crashing into aquarium walls because their nature is to range widely. They swim far to stalk their prey, and they move continually to keep water flowing through their gills. Aquarium tanks just aren't big enough. What's more, their favorite menu item is live prey that they themselves pursue and catch. They generally turn up their noses at aquarium food. And even when great whites are returned to the sea, some will die from the stress of the change in environment.

RECORD-SIZE FISH, RECORD-SIZE AQUARIUMS

The Georgia Aquarium in Atlanta is the world's largest. And it holds the biggest captive shark—and the world's largest fish—the whale shark. It can grow to 42 feet (13 m) long, close to the size of a semitrailer. The entrance to the Ocean Voyager tank at the Georgia Aquarium in Atlanta is a tunnel with a curving acrylic ceiling looking up into the tank. It's pretty—like being in a tropical fish tank—and multicolored and sparkly. At the end of the long tunnel, visitors enter a room with a 2,361-foot (720 m) transparent wall looking into a 6.3 million-gallon (24 million L) tank. They find a place to sit or lean, and they wait a minute. There's a gasp.

This whale shark feeds on small fish in the Arafura Sea off the western coast of the island of New Guinea. Many sharks, including the whale shark, do not thrive in captivity. They become bored and depressed. Some quickly become sick and die.

Everybody points. Kids run along the edge of the tank to keep up. With what? A deep blue-gray whale shark, speckled in white, with an entourage of remoras.

The Ocean Voyager gallery is home to four whale sharks. For a fee of more than $200, visitors can even swim in the tank with the gorgeous giants. Maintaining the aquarium's reputation as a healthy second-home environment for massive whale sharks has had its problems, though. Ralph and Norton were the first of the aquarium's whale sharks. A commercial fishing fleet in Taiwan had caught them as bycatch in 2005. The aquarium bought them and flew them by airplane to Atlanta. They died in early 2007 after staff treated their tank with a chemical to reduce parasites.

The death of the whale sharks—and problems raising healthy beluga whale calves born in captivity at the aquarium—has raised difficult questions. Is the strain on the individual animals and the sorrow of losing them worth what we learn about them? Scott Higley is the vice president of external affairs at the Georgia Aquarium. He says the aquarium's goal is edutainment, education about whale sharks and the entertainment and joy of seeing their awesome gorgeousness. He feels the trade-offs are worth it.

Despite controversy, aquariums continue to keep sharks in captivity. By 2016 Churaumi Aquarium had a new pair of whale sharks—a male and a female. The aquarium curator, Keichii Sato, an expert on captive care, speculated about whether the two would mate. If they did—and if they produced a baby whale shark—it would become the first time that whale shark mating and birthing is observed, in captivity or in the wild.

PICK ONE FROM THE CATALOG

Researchers and aquarists get to know sharks by site. They recognize individual markings and personalities. And to organize what they know about these individual sharks, researchers have developed shark catalogs. Whale catalogs rely on the distinctive tail fluke markings of humpback whales to identify individual humpbacks. Ichthyologists rely on photographs and listings to keep track of individual sharks and their movements.

One of the biggest shark catalogs is Wildbook. In 1995 marine conservation biologist Brad Norman of Murdoch University in Perth, Australia, established Ecocean, an organization for studying whale sharks. Job number one was to find a way to tell whale sharks apart, and the key lay in the spots on their bodies.

Norman realized he could use the distinctive pattern of spots to identify individual whale sharks. He worked with information architect Jason Holmberg to develop a computer program to help match spot patterns in photographs with specific sharks. Holmberg borrowed an algorithm used by astronomers to scan the sky. Instead of stars, Ecocean uses spots. Wildbook has grown to include a collection of more than fifty thousand photographs of whale sharks, which researchers use to track where the sharks swim.

What's more, Ecocean's Wildbook database accepts anyone's shark photographs. So a scuba diver or snorkeler or boater can photograph a whale shark, submit pictures, and see if they get a match. Since shark scientists can't be everywhere, this program connects them with people all over the world—and with whale sharks tagged or untagged wherever they're found. What if your whale shark isn't in the catalog? Then this new, unknown individual will need a name for the catalog. You may even get to name it!

Researchers also study dead sharks caught by commercial fishing fleets. Fishers haul dead sharks to necropsy labs. There, biologists examine the dead animals for many studies, including external morphology, anatomy, diet, and reproduction. They take size measurements, note the animal's sex, and consider the number of sharks a fleet has caught. They record the capture location, maturity stage, stomach contents, and presence of parasites and any embryos a female may be carrying. The data from fishing fleets helps scientists better understand where and how deep in the ocean certain species live and whether they live in groups related to species, sex, size, and/ or age. Yes, they get similar data from tagging sharks themselves. But the more eyes in the ocean—and the more sharks observed—the better the scientific understanding of how sharks use their environments.

SHARK GENES

In late 2017, the marine biology community got big news: the completion of the sequencing of a great white shark genome (a map of the shark's genes). Other projects for fully identifying and sequencing (or mapping) shark genomes are under way, including the genes of whale sharks. Genome sequencing is a historically new development in science.

STUMPY AND ZORRO

Stumpy and Zorro were the guinea pigs—the test animals—for the first entries in the Wildbook catalog. Their distinctive spots and Stumpy's damaged tail (the source of his name) set them apart from other male whale sharks. Brad Norman, founder of Ecocean and cocreator of Wildbook, told ABC Australia television, "These two, they've been coming back [to the protected waters of Ningaloo Marine Park off the coast of Western Australia] for such a long time, and we've been able to see the progression through to maturity, we think these two big boys have been out there mating and might be the father of many."

DNA is the basic chemical ingredient of animal genes. Long strands of DNA on chromosomes spiral within animal cells. DNA dictates the type of organism and cells that will develop in a life-form, how its cells will grow and change, what the organism will look like, and how it will behave and function. The sequence of genes on chromosomes can take years to map out. That's because there are so many of them—from thousands to millions to billions. The first sequenced genome in history was a super-simple virus, in 1976. Twenty years later, scientists mapped a yeast genome. In 2000 a fruit fly. In 2003 scientists with the international Human Genome Project completed the human genome, mapping nineteen thousand to twenty thousand human genes. So why is it taking so long for sharks?

The answer? The great white shark genome is 1.6 times bigger than the human genome. That's because sharks have been on Earth for so much longer than humans have—more than four hundred million years, compared to only six million years for humans. So sharks have changed and responded to millions of years' worth of additional challenges. That means they also have more genetic material. And among the shark's advanced genetic capabilities is the ability to resist cancer.

How did scientists discover this? Mahmood Shivji and a team of researchers already knew that cuts and other open wounds on shark and ray skin start healing in just a few hours. This quick rate of healing is much faster than in any mammal. Shivji knew that studying the shark immune system—its network of cells, tissues, and organs for fighting disease—would provide clues about fast healing. So he began to look at shark-healing genes and found two that seem to impact healing as well as resistance to cancer. Shivji and his team hope that further study will produce techniques for curing or even preventing cancers in people.

8

CITIZEN SCIENCE FOR THE SHARKS

"ZERO-DATA" IS DOCUMENTING THE ABSENCE OF
SOMETHING—IN THIS CASE, SHARKS. AND THIS DATA
IS VITAL FOR THE SHARKSCOUNT PROGRAM. . . . IF
YOU GO ON A DIVE AND SEE NO SHARKS, PLEASE
RECORD THAT DIVE ON YOUR DATASHEET AND
REPORT IT TO US. ALL YOUR DIVING INFORMATION
IS VALUABLE.

—MICHAEL BEAR, CITIZEN SCIENCE PROJECT DIRECTOR, OCEAN
SANCTUARIES, SAN DIEGO, CALIFORNIA

t Lake Travis at Volente Beach Water Park in Leander, Texas, audiences float in inflated inner tubes to watch a movie. Yep, it's a swim-up movie! And it's none other than *Jaws*. Sharks still make the hair rise on the back of many people's necks. Yet various factors

Shark tourism is on the rise. These scuba divers in a shark-viewing cage watch a great white shark in the Pacific Ocean off Mexico's Guadalupe Island.

have raised interest in and love of sharks—from the documentaries of Jacques Cousteau; the popularity of aquariums; the work of ichthyologists such as Eugenie Clark, Robert Hueter, Chris Lowe, Simon Thorrold, and Greg Skomal; to the increase of recreational scuba diving and snorkeling. Discovery Channel's yearly Shark Week is part of the fun too.

New technologies including acoustic tagging and animal-borne cameras allow researchers to unlock the mysteries of sharks' lives, which they can then share with the public through social media. Whew! While some people may always be terrified of sharks, many more have come to understand that sharks and their superpowers are not so scary after all. In fact, they are vital to the health of our oceans and therefore of our shared planet.

2018 was a record year for shark attacks in the U.S.: **53**.* (One was fatal.) More people (38) were killed by dog bites.⊙

* International Shark Attack File
⊙ DogsBite.org

Shark populations are in decline (dropping). Close to 100 million△ sharks are killed each year — many for their fins, which people eat.

△ Marine Policy

These days, **you** can follow great white sharks around if you want, thanks to the ap Global Shark Tracker and a ship called OCEARCH.

OCEARCH has a hydraulic platform that lifts in and out of the ocean. **Chris Fisher** and his crew attach tags that track a shark's path through the sea.

1. SHARK BITES ON A LINE WITH FLOATS, IS REELED IN.

2. PLATFORM IS RAISED, LIFTS SHARK OUT OF WATER.

3. STOPWATCH BEGINS: **15** MINUTES FOR BLOOD SAMPLES AND ULTRASOUND TEST TO ASSESS CONDITION. SATELLITE TAG ATTACHED TO DORSAL FIN.

4. PLATFORM DROPS. SHARK SWIMS FREE.

Biologist **Simon Thorrold**, (of Woods Hole Oceanographic Institution) who uses data from the OCEARCH work, says,

"In the past, what we learned about great white sharks, we learned from dead ones. New tagging techniques let us get into the lives of sharks without killing them. **People** are having daily conversations about where these sharks are."

Along with new technology, shark scientists have another major tool to rely on: a public that is fascinated by sharks and that uses the Internet to connect. As citizen scientists realize what sharks are up against, they are putting aside their fears and changing activities that are harmful to sharks. They are also using their senses and learning new skills with new tools to add valuable information to scientist databases.

How can you help sharks? Go look for some!

No joke. For example, citizen divers and snorkelers share their observations, smartphone pictures, and GoPro videos with scientists, who add this information to their data. As new technologies develop, such as drones, early adopters share what they find with experts. Having all these extra eyes and cameras over and under the sea saves scientists time, effort, and money. The information helps ichthyologists confirm—and protect— shark habitat.

Some citizen scientists are also helping researchers tag sharks. Tagging helps scientists figure out where sharks go. Establishing shark habitat gives fisheries a better idea of when and if shark fishing is impacting the animal's populations and by how much. Are fleets fishing too many sharks? Or are they limiting their catch to be sure to maintain a healthy shark population? Habitat information is also key to figuring out which areas of the ocean should be set aside as marine sanctuaries. These protected areas are safe for sharks and for people who want to see them. Sanctuaries limit fishing, hunting, shipping, boating, and other human uses to keep environments as natural as possible for wildlife.

SHARK FISHING FOR SCIENCE

Recreational and commercial fishers team up with researchers from the Cooperative Shark Tagging Program (CSTP), a project run by the National Marine Fisheries Service (NMFS). Together they study shark species of the Atlantic Ocean. The recreational fishers catch sharks, usually with rod and reel. They attach Rototags (small plastic identification tags) to the fins for recording the shark's species, size, and location. Usually commercial fishers

Nancy Kohler, head of the Apex Predators Program (part of the Cooperative Shark Tagging Program), captures a tiger shark during a research survey.

end up recatching the tagged animals as bycatch in nets or with lines, and they know to report on the tags to the Cooperative Shark Tagging Program. Biologists and volunteer observers sometimes recatch the tagged sharks too, usually with rod and reel.

Scientists with the NMFS compare the locations of tagging and recatch to understand shark migrations. Besides the distance the animals travel (and some idea of route), the data aids scientists in figuring out shark diversity (which species are where), and abundance (how many of each kind are in an area). Information about shark age, growth, and mortality also help researchers understand a typical shark's life span.

The Cooperative Shark Tagging Program began in 1962. Scientists recruited one hundred volunteers, and by 2013, they have tagged more than 243,000 sharks of fifty-two species. They had also recaptured more than 14,000 sharks of thirty-three species. A sandbar shark holds the record for the longest time between tagging and recapture—27.8 years. The record for distance traveled goes to a blue shark, recaught 3,997 nautical miles from where it was first tagged. (A nautical mile is equal to 1.15 miles, or 1.85 km, so this is 4,600 miles, or 7,402 km.)

SO YOU'VE CAUGHT A SHARK . . .

Then what?

Hopefully, you and your crew have some Rototags on board—and a guide to shark species. The National Marine Fisheries Service prints and laminates shark guides to help anglers know what they've caught and how and where to accurately tag the catch (on the dorsal fin). The fisheries service website advises to tag only the species you can accurately identify. Read the site's tips on figuring out what sex the shark is so you can record that information too.

If you're out to tag sharks, be sure to use the right type of hook. And stick close to recommended fishing practices to maximize a shark's chance of surviving the catch-and-release experience.

What if the shark is already tagged? The fisheries service advises that you and your team gather the following information:

- tag number
- species and sex
- date of capture
- location (latitude and longitude) of catch
- length in meters and weight in kilograms
- fishing method (how the shark was caught, whether with a net, surf casting, or deep-sea fishing)
- whether the shark was kept or released alive

After you've collected this information,

- call (877) 826-2612 toll-free or
- e-mail the information to sharkrecap@noaa.gov or
- mail it to:
  Cooperative Shark Tagging Program
  NOAA's National Marine Fisheries Service
  28 Tarzwell Drive
  Narragansett, RI 02882

MONSTERS IN DANGER

Not everyone who catches a shark is doing so for the benefit of science and education. In 2015 the *Guardian* newspaper reported that towns in the East Coast of the United States still host seventy-one well-attended monster tournaments. Corporations typically sponsor these competitions where sports people catch and kill large pelagic sharks including porbeagle, mako, and threshers. They hang them on giant hooks on docks to show off their catch. The prize money goes to the person who catches the biggest specimen. Officials with the National Oceanographic and Atmospheric Administration (NOAA) and the International Union for Conservation of Nature (IUCN) say the tournaments are okay. The number of catches is limited, and populations of sharks in the areas where tournaments take place are large enough to stay healthy.

Yet marine ecologist Sarah Fowler, former chair of the IUCN's Shark Specialist Group, told the *Guardian*, "It seems inappropriate for big commercial sponsors to be sponsoring the killing of a threatened species when it's not necessary. You can have tag-and-release tournaments instead and thereby contribute to research programs." And Sharon Young, the marine issues coordinator for the Humane Society of the United States, told the *Atlantic* magazine that seeing dead sharks for only entertainment bothers her because "we understand that they are a fragile species."

A BIGGER THRILL

Some citizens feel they are helping preserve sharks through ecotourism. These trips focus on vacations to places with an intriguing ecosystem. For example, people wanting to scuba dive with hammerhead sharks will vacation close to waters where the sharks live. The tourists pay for hotels, food, souvenirs, and activities in the local community and contribute to the local economy. *National Geographic* magazine estimates that the existence of one live hammerhead shark in the wild in Costa Rica's Cocos Island brings in $1.6 million a year from ecotourists who want to see it. So a single live shark is far more valuable than a single dead shark, which is worth about

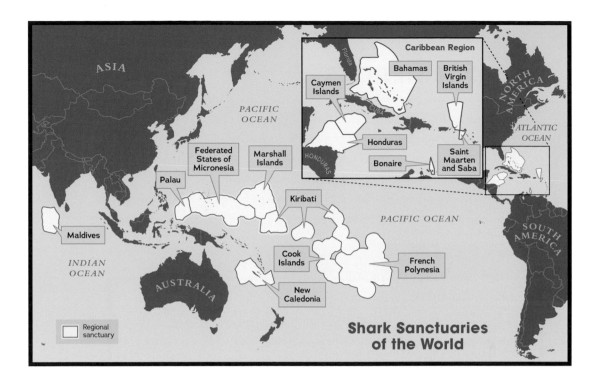

Regional sanctuary

Shark Sanctuaries of the World

$200 to a fisher selling it at market. Thousands of scuba divers come to the sanctuary at Palau to see grey reef sharks, bringing about $2 million to the community every year. When caught by fishers, the dead sharks are worth about $108 apiece. Yet fishing fleets need the income they earn from their work, so tension exists between the fishing industry and ecotourism.

Shark-related tourism more than doubled since the late 1990s, growing to $314 million a year in the second decade of the twenty-first century. It is projected to more than double in the next twenty years, to $780 million a year. Meanwhile, the worldwide shark fishing industry (worth $630 million annually) is in decline because of increasing pressure to conserve sharks. So fisheries economist Andrés Cisneros-Montemayor of the University of British Colombia in Vancouver predicts that shark ecotourism will soon be worth more than global shark fisheries. "The emerging shark tourism industry attracts nearly 600,000 shark watchers annually, directly supporting 10,000 jobs," he says. "Leaving sharks in the ocean is worth much more than putting them on the menu."

LOCAL HEROES

Ecotourism is one way of preserving sharks. A program in Bimini, a chain of islands in the Bahamas, takes things a few steps further. The Watermen Project, collaborating with the Bimini Biological Field Station Sharklab, invites teenagers to tag great hammerhead sharks and bull sharks. The teens are also trained to take muscle samples from the fish. The work involves skills that many people in Bimini already have. They know how to spearfish with precision and how to free dive (dive without a scuba tank). So they are

JOIN THE GILLS CLUB!

The Gills Club is a group of women who "live like every week is Shark Week." Founded in 2014, the group works to inspire girls to work on shark science and connect with adult female shark researchers. Members include girls of every age, including young shark fans and teen aquarium volunteers. It also includes professional scientists such as Vicky Vásquez of the Pacific Shark Research Center in Moss Landing, California. Membership is free. The Gills Club blog includes posts from scientists in the field and in the lab, and advice on becoming a shark scientist.

Members of the Gills Club get an up-close look at a dogfish shark. They are learning from female scientists how to dissect the shark to learn more about its anatomy.

excellent at approaching sharks without scaring them. The teens use a dart gun to attach an acoustic tag to each shark. Acoustic receivers planted on the seafloor pick up the pings from the transmitters to show which sharks are where. The teens also use a biopsy gun to snatch a muscle sample so that scientists can analyze the shark's DNA.

In her work with sharks, South African marine biologist Alison Kock uses knowledge she picked up as a kid. "When I was very young," she recalls, "I used to accompany my dad on boat trips to harvest crayfish. We would spend hours at sea, deploying nets and waiting for the crayfish to climb inside. When we retrieved the nets, it wasn't only crayfish that we found, but small sharks too. The little sharks would curl up into a ball with their tail covering their eyes and my dad instructed me to kiss them on the head and gently release them back into the water. When I did so, the shy sharks would uncurl and swim back down to the bottom." As a student in college, seeing a great white shark launch itself 6.5 feet (2 m) into the air to nab a seal convinced her she'd found her research topic. As an adult, Kock not only studies great whites in False Bay, South Africa, she is also the project leader for the Save Our Seas Foundation. This organization works to protect life in the ocean, especially rays and sharks.

Alison Kock also attaches tags and Crittercam cameras to the fins of great whites as part of her scientific work. And she manages the shore-based Shark Spotters Programme in Cape Town, South Africa. Started in 2004, the program employs people to spot sharks for research as well as to protect swimmers at area beaches. Her program was among the first in the world to train and hire citizen scientists.

Cape Town is home to four million people, including lots of water-loving folks who kayak, surf, windsurf, kiteboard, dive, and fish along the rugged, gorgeous coast. The Atlantic Ocean there is home to great white, bull, and tiger sharks, among the most aggressive shark species. The members of the Shark Spotters Programme use binoculars to monitor beaches at nearby Table Mountain, the main feature of the popular national park of the same name. Shark spotters keep an eye out for sharks, using a

Shark Spotters "Be Shark Smart" posters are on South African ocean beaches to provide safety tips and information about how to behave appropriately in waters where sharks live.

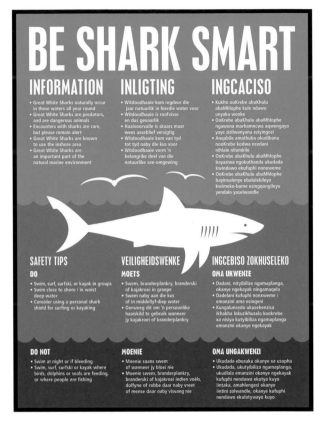

BE SHARK SMART

INFORMATION
- Great White Sharks naturally occur in these waters all year round
- Great White Sharks are predators, and are dangerous animals
- Encounters with sharks are rare, but please remain alert
- Great White Sharks are known to use the inshore area
- Great White Sharks are an important part of the natural marine environment

INLIGTING
- Witdoodhaaie kom regdeur die jaar natuurlik in hierdie water voor
- Witdoodhaaie is roofvisse en dus gevaarlik
- Haaivoorvalle is skaars maar wees asseblief versigtig
- Witdoodhaaie kom van tyd tot tyd naby die kus voor
- Witdoodhaaie vorm 'n belangrike deel van die natuurlike see-omgewing

INGCACISO
- Kukho ooKrebe abaKhulu abaMhlophe kule ndawo unyaka wonke
- OoKrebe abaKhulu abaMhlophe ngawona marhamncwa aqwengayo yaye zizilwanyana eziyingozi
- Anqabile amathuba okudibana nooKrebe kodwa ncedani nihlale nilumkile
- OoKrebe abaKhulu abaMhlophe bayaziwa ngokuthanda ukudada kwindawo ekufuphi nonxweme
- OoKrebe abaKhulu abaMhlophe bayinxalenye ebalulekileyo kwimeko-bume esingqongileyo yendalo yaselwandle

SAFETY TIPS
DO
- Swim, surf, surfski or kayak in groups
- Swim close to shore / in waist deep water
- Consider using a personal shark shield for surfing or kayaking

VEILIGHEIDSWENKE
MOETS
- Swem, branderplankry, branderski of kajakroei in groepe
- Swem naby aan die kus of in middellyf-diep water
- Oorweeg dit om 'n persoonlike haaiskild te gebruik wanneer jy kajakroei of branderplankry

INGCEBISO ZOKHUSELEKO
OMA UKWENZE
- Dadani, nityibilize ngamaplanga, okanye ngekayak ningamaqela
- Dadelani kufuphi nonxweme / emanzini ama esingeni
- Kungaluncedo ukusebenzisa ikhakha lokuzikhusela kookrebe xa nisiya kutyibiliza ngamaplanga emanzini okanye ngekayak

DO NOT
- Swim at night or if bleeding
- Swim, surf, surfski or kayak where birds, dolphins or seals are feeding, or where people are fishing

MOENIE
- Moenie saans swem of wanneer jy bloei nie
- Moenie swem, branderplankry, branderski of kajakroei indien voëls, dolfyne of robbe daar naby vreet of mense daar naby visvang nie

OMA UNGAKWENZI
- Ukudada ebusuku okanye xa usopha
- Ukudada, ukutyibiliza ngamaplanga, ukudlala emanzini okanye ngekayak kufuphi nendawo ekutya kuyo iintaka, amahlengesi okanye iintini zolwandle, okanye kufuphi nendawo ekulotywayo kuyo

flag to advise beachgoers of the level of shark risk. For example, a white flag with a black shark on it means the beach is closed because a shark is in the water. One of the goals of the Shark Spotters Programme is to prevent harmful incidents between sharks and humans so that the public attitude toward great whites will improve. A more positive understanding of sharks is an important part of shark conservation.

"In the beginning, back in 2004, most of us knew very little about shark behavior in False Bay, and we came a long way. . . . Now the public is very supportive and it is just from time to time that we get one or two people who are arrogant or ignorant and ignore our calls," says Monwabisi Sikweyiya, a lifeguard and one of the program's first spotters. Sikweyiya is Shark Spotters' field manager. His advice in case you unintentionally encounter a shark in the water? "Don't paddle, just float. If you're lucky enough, the animal will just swim away. But white sharks are ambush animals; they can take you by surprise." In 2016 Shark Spotters began work on a new app that will let beachgoers check conditions before setting out for the shore.

GOOD EYES

Data gathered by nonscientists is proving to be very reliable and is becoming an increasingly vital contribution to the understanding of the world of sharks. Citizen scientists are helping fill in some of the blanks. For example, in 2014 Gabriel Vianna and his associates at the University of Western Australia, Perth, learned that the IUCN had categorized almost half of the 1,041 known species of elasmobranchs (sharks and rays) as Data Deficient. This means that ichthyologists don't know enough about their abundance (numbers) or distribution (habitat range) to determine the health and stability of individual elasmobranchs species. The IUCN makes designations about the conservation status of Earth's animals, from Not Evaluated and Data Deficient all the way to Endangered and Extinct. Nations around the globe make decisions about whether and how to protect their oceans, based in part on IUCN rankings. Icthyologists therefore feel pressure to come up with better information to help the IUCN and nations make their decisions about animal life on Earth.

SHARK TRUTH
More people are killed every year by falling coconuts in Asia than by sharks around the world.

The Perth scientists were studying grey reef sharks in Palau. They decided to bring in citizen scientists to help with their project. So Vianna's group asked local dive guides to observe and count sharks. They also asked them to gather information about the strength of the sea current and the temperature of the water. Telemetry (automated communications) buoys in the area would measure this same type of information. Vianna's group wanted to know if the data from the divers and the buoys would match. And would the presence of divers in the waters scare sharks away or tempt them to come close?

The data was good news for the divers. It showed that their presence in the water neither frightened away nor attracted sharks. The presence of sharks varied according to sea conditions. So, in rough waters, divers saw few if any sharks. In calm waters, they saw more. And it was good news for scientists too. The results from the acoustic technology and from the divers were comparable. So the data gathered by nonscientists was reliable, and scientists could use it in their shark assessments.

In other areas of ocean science and in other parts of the ocean, citizen observations have been a big help. For example, the Reef Environmental Education Foundation (REEF) uses data gathered by divers and snorkelers to determine the health of reef ecosystems. They report on invasive species such as lionfish, which can destroy reefs. When lionfish are located, efforts to remove them can begin. On Atlantic and Gulf of Mexico beaches that attract sea turtles, volunteer monitors gather data about the turtles as they emerge from the ocean to dig the sandy nests in which they lay their eggs. The volunteers also protect the nests from people or animals that try to dig them up. And along the bluffs of California's Pacific coast, whale watchers with binoculars keep an eye on migrating gray whales. Increasingly, scientists are finding ways to involve citizen scientists in new research.

Citizen scientists include tourists watching the waters along coastlines, from cliff tops, or from boats and sharing what they see with experts.

BE A SHARK SCIENTIST

Scientist Catherine McDonald does her shark research at the Shark Research and Conservation Program at the University of Miami in Coral Gables, Florida. There she trains interns to handle and care for sharks. For people who want to study sharks as a career, she suggests that budding ichthyologists learn to be skilled swimmers, divers, and boaters. And she encourages them to volunteer at aquariums to get accustomed to working with animals. She emphasizes the importance of being good at working as part of a team, listening well, and doing your job with careful attention. Good manners count too. It's important to be polite and respectful as you work with and for others, and it can make the difference in getting—or not—the role, job, or opportunity you want.

SPYING ON SEVENGILLS

Michael Bear started one of the world's first citizen science shark projects. In 2009 he began hearing a lot more big fish stories than he ever had before. From divers in the San Diego area, he was hearing stories about sightings of data-deficient broadnose sevengill sharks. He realized the stories might be true. "I was diving off of Point La Jolla when a large seven footer [2 m] sevengill shark glided majestically between me and my dive buddy, who was no more than two meters [7 feet] away from me," Bear wrote. "To say we were startled would be an understatement." Sevengills are a shallow-swimming shark usually found near shore. Fishers were catching them, but this species was unprotected because not enough was known about them. So, in 2010, Bear founded the Sevengill Shark Identification Project to turn divers' stories into data. He hired Vallorie Hodges, an expert on diving with sharks, as the project's lead scientist.

The first step was to invite citizen divers to photograph the head and gills of sharks in the wild without endangering their own (or the sharks') safety. An essential part of the project was to figure out how to then collect and organize information and photographs coming in by the Internet from divers. For help, Bear consulted Jason Holmberg—the same information architect who had worked with marine biologist Brad Norman and Ecocean on whale shark photo identifications for Wildbook. Holmberg expanded his software-driven Wildbook database to give citizens an open-source (copyright-free) platform for uploading and sharing their snapshots and sightings of sevengill sharks. As with whale sharks, this version of Wildbook analyzes spots on shark bodies. If it confirms the distinctive black freckles around the sevengill's eyes, the program can make a positive identification of each individual shark.

Together, the divers and scientists generated databases of photos, videos, and identifications. The work went so well in San Diego that ichthyologists and citizen scientists in False Bay adopted the project to track sevengills there. The smartphone app Sevengill Shark Tracker also helps scientists gather more data quickly.

PLAYING TO THE CROWD

Bear went on to launch Ocean Sanctuaries in 2014 with recreational and science diver Barbara Lloyd. The ocean conservation organization is focused on species conservation, ocean sustainability, and citizen science projects. It also makes documentary films about the ocean. Ocean Sanctuaries invites citizen scientists to use an online mapping tool called FieldScope to upload images and data about leopard, horn, angel, tope, blue, mako, great white, and thresher sharks. They say, "Surprise us!"

Crowd-sourced research, or information gathered online from many people, contributes to growing sites such as the Encyclopedia of Life (EOL). The main goal of EOL is to combine scientist and citizen images and information to create a page for every species on Earth. Anyone with photographs and information about sharks (or other animals) can share them there. Before the EOL site will post them, scientists vet them to confirm the contributor's observations. So far, EOL has close to 5.6 million pages. Citizen science organizations such as Shark Stewards in California work with iNaturalist, an online social network of scientists and citizens committed to preserving biodiversity. Together, they collect and share data about sharks and rays. The site has observations of more than one hundred thousand species by more than one hundred thousand observers worldwide.

THE LATEST SHARK

Stop the presses! A new shark species has been discovered! In a study led by Florida International University, ichthyologists determined in 2016 that they had found a new species of bonnethead shark, a type of hammerhead shark. Scientists studying bonnetheads in the Caribbean waters off the coast of Belize realized that the genes of the bonnetheads in this area differ from bonnetheads in other parts of the Caribbean and in the Atlantic. The IUCN lists bonnetheads as of Least Concern because they are abundant. But the realization that bonnetheads in Belize are a different species altogether calls this label into question. A closer look may reveal that so few of this newly discovered species exist that it requires protection of its habitat.

"Determining when you have a new species is a tricky thing," study author Demian Chapman told *Mental Floss* magazine. "But these sharks are living in a separate environment from their fellow bonnetheads, and they're likely on their own evolutionary trajectory."

Discoveries such as these were once made only by scientists. But as citizens worldwide become more involved in observations of wildlife and as conservation efforts improve the world for sharks, scientists are moving over to make room for—and invite—contributions from shark lovers everywhere. After all, the more we know about sharks—and the less we are ruled by fears not based in reality—the more we can love, value, and protect them.

SHARK GUIDE

The world's oceans are home to eight identified orders of sharks, with thirty-one families that include a total of about 479 shark species. As ichthyologists discover previously unknown species, the number of species changes. Biological classification of sharks also evolves as researchers gain a new and better understanding of shark morphology (body shape) and genetics (underlying species relationships). This Shark Guide lists the eight orders with one example species for each. To learn more about other sharks within each order, go to the Encyclopedia of Life (www.eol.org) or SharkSider (www.sharksider.com).

The IUCN Red List is the gold standard of conservation status. The organization ranks an animal's status in order of seven risk levels of extinction: Least Concern, Near Threatened, Vulnerable, Endangered, Critically Endangered, Extinct in the Wild, or Extinct. The IUCN labels some species as Data Deficient because scientists don't yet have enough information about the animals to make a determination. Other species may be listed as Not Evaluated if the animals have not been studied yet. The rankings in this Shark Guide are from the IUCN Red List. (If you are wondering whether there's more room for shark scientists, the answer is *yes*!)

CARCHARHINIFORMES

These ground sharks include 270 species, such as hammerheads, catsharks, blue, tiger, lemon, and whitetip sharks. Scyliorhinidae (catsharks) are one of the largest families of this type of shark, with about 160 species. Ground sharks all have nictitating eyelids, a mouth positioned behind the front of their eyes, five pairs of gill slits, an anal fin, and two spineless dorsal fins.

BLUE SHARK

SCIENTIFIC NAME	*Prionace glauca*
HABITAT	found in all the world's oceans, from the surface to waters 1,150 feet (350 m) deep
LENGTH	maximum recorded size up to 13 feet (4 m)
WEIGHT	up to 450 pounds (204 kg)
DIET	small bony fish and invertebrates, such as squid; also dead mammals
FEATURES	named for the shark's vivid blue color
STATUS	Near Threatened

HETERODONTIFORMES

The 9 species of bullheaded, or horn, sharks are found in the Indian and Pacific Oceans. Bullheaded sharks all have a piggish snout, a sharp eyebrow-like ridge above the eye, a small mouth well forward of their eyes, spined dorsal fins, and an anal fin.

CRESTED BULLHEAD SHARK

SCIENTIFIC NAME	*Heterodontus galeatus*
HABITAT	bottom-dwelling, living off the coast of eastern Australia
LENGTH	maximum recorded size of 3.9 feet (1.2 m)
WEIGHT	undocumented
DIET	mollusks, sea urchins, and small bony fish
FEATURES	slow moving, lurk in undersea caves, and feed at night
STATUS	Least Concern

HEXANCHIFORMES

The frilled and cow sharks include six- and seven-gill sharks such as the broadnose sevengill and the bluntnose six-gill. Hexanchidae (cow sharks) include 37 species. Hexanchiformes, considered the most primitive sharks, all have six or seven pairs of gill slits, one dorsal fin (set low on their backs), one anal fin, a low caudal fin, and large, teardrop-shaped eyes.

SHARPNOSE SEVENGILL

SCIENTIFIC NAME	*Heptranchias perlo*
HABITAT	deep waters almost everywhere except the northern Pacific Ocean
LENGTH	maximum recorded size of 4.6 feet (1.4 m)
WEIGHT	maximum weight of 236 pounds (107 kg)
DIET	small bony fish, shellfish, invertebrates such as mollusks, and small sharks and rays
FEATURES	green eyes and jagged upper teeth to grip thrashing prey
STATUS	Near Threatened

LAMNIFORMES

The mackerel sharks are a varied group of big and big-mouthed sharks that includes basking, great white, shortfin mako, thresher, sand tiger, goblin, and megamouth sharks. The 15 species comprise a fraction of the hundreds of lamniformes that have come and gone. The family Odontospididae (sand tiger sharks) has 4 species. Mackerel sharks have no nictitating eyelids, a mouth positioned behind the front of their eyes, five pairs of gill slits, an anal fin, and two spineless dorsal fins.

PORBEAGLE

SCIENTIFIC NAME	*Lamna nasus*
HABITAT	found mostly in the 30°N to 70°N and 30°S to 50°S latitudes in all oceans
LENGTH	12 feet (3.5 m)
WEIGHT	298 pounds (135 kg)
DIET	cephalopods (squid and octopus) and bony fish
FEATURES	known by the white spot at the base of the dorsal fin
STATUS	Vulnerable

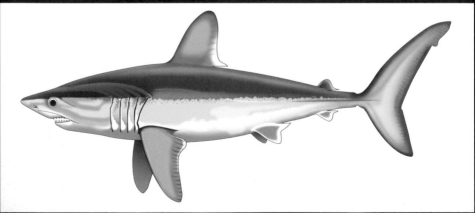

ORECTOLOBIFORMES

The carpet sharks are a diverse group of 39 species of sharks. They include whale, nurse, zebra, bamboo, and wobbegong sharks. Carpet sharks all have a mouth completely in front of their eyes, two spineless dorsal fins, an anal fin, and five pairs of gill slits. Except for the whale shark, they are all bottom-dwellers and have a spiracle below each eye to help with breathing. The whale shark's spiracles are to the rear of each eye. Most carpet sharks live in the Indian Ocean or the western Pacific Ocean. Whale sharks live in tropical and warm temperate waters worldwide.

NURSE SHARK

SCIENTIFIC NAME	*Ginglymostoma cirratum*
HABITAT	subtropical and tropical Atlantic and Pacific Oceans
LENGTH	maximum recorded size of 10 feet (3 m)
WEIGHT	up to 330 pounds (150 kg)
DIET	little fish, snails and other mollusks, and crustaceans
FEATURES	makes sucking sounds while hunting in the sand
STATUS	Data Deficient

PRISTIOPHORIFORMES

The saw sharks comprise 8 species. They all have a saw—a flattened, bladelike snout edged in teeth. Saw sharks have spiracles for breathing, dorsal fins without spines, nasal barbels, and five or six pairs of gill slits. They have no anal fin.

COMMON SAW SHARK

SCIENTIFIC NAME	*Pristiophorus cirratus*
HABITAT	the underwater continental shelf along the coast of southern Australia
LENGTH	maximum size of 5 feet (1.5 m)
WEIGHT	19 pounds (8.6 kg)
DIET	fish, squid, and crustaceans
FEATURES	bottom-dwellers with extra-long nasal barbels the shape of mustaches for sensing buried prey
STATUS	Least Concern

SQUALIFORMES

The dogfish sharks live mostly at the bottom of the deep sea. They are the second-largest order of sharks, with 119 species. The family Squalidae, the spiny dogfish sharks, live in shallower waters. Dogfish sharks all have a spine along the forward edge of their dorsal fins, large almond-shaped eyes, and a large spiracle behind each eye. Many dogfish are bioluminescent, producing their own light.

SPINY **DOGFISH**

SCIENTIFIC NAME	Squalus acanthias
HABITAT	along the coasts of Europe, the United States, Canada, New Zealand, and Chile diving as deep as 2,900 feet (884 m) in winter
LENGTH	up to 49 inches, or 124 cm (females), and 39 inches, or 99 cm (males)
WEIGHT	females from 7.1 to 9.9 pounds (3.2 to 4.5 kg); smaller and lighter males
DIET	schooling fish such as herring and capelin as well as jellyfish and squid
FEATURES	the longest pregnancy of any vertebrate, twenty-two to twenty-four months
STATUS	Vulnerable

SQUATINIFORMES

The 19 species of angel sharks include the family Somniosidae, the "sleeping sharks." Angel sharks have flattened bodies, large front heads with skin flaps, raylike mouths, nasal barbels, and no anal fin.

GREENLAND SHARK

SCIENTIFIC NAME	*Somniosus microcephalus*
HABITAT	North Atlantic and Arctic Oceans
LENGTH	maximum recorded size of 21 feet (6.4 m)
WEIGHT	up to 3,100 pounds (1,406 kg)
DIET	voracious appetite; eels, fish, other sharks, and carrion (dead animals), even moose and reindeer remains discovered in their stomach
FEATURES	the longest life span of all vertebrate species, up to 500 years or more and takes 150 years to reach sexual maturity; Greenland shark flesh, nontoxic when dried but poisonous when fresh
STATUS	Near Threatened

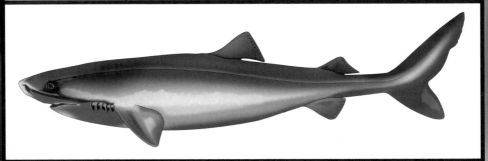

SOURCE NOTES

4   Alessandro De Maddalena and Walter Heim, *Sharks of New England* (Camden, ME: Down East, 2010), preface.

4–5   Peter Benchley and Karen Wojtyla, *Shark Life: True Stories about Sharks and the Sea* (New York: Random House, 2007), 3.

8   Ibid., 1–2.

8   Ibid.

8   Ibid., 47–48.

10   Dan Stone, "100 Million Sharks Killed Every Year, Study Shows on Eve of International Conference on Shark Protection," *National Geographic*, March 1, 2013, http://voices.nationalgeographic.com/2013/03/01/100-million-sharks-killed -every-year-study-shows-on-eve-of-international-conference-on-shark-protection/.

13   Katherine Nichols, "Sharks as 'Aumakua,'" *Honolulu Advertiser*, January 14, 2001, https://www.moolelo.com/sharks.html.

15   Julia K. Baum, Ransom A. Myers, Daniel G. Kehler, Boris Worm, Shelton J. Harley, and Penny A. Doherty, "Collapse and Conservation of Shark Populations in the Northwest Atlantic," *Science* 299, no. 5605 (January 17, 2003): 389–392, http:// science.sciencemag.org/content/sci/299/5605/389.full.pdf.

18   Ashley Fetters, "The Evolution of Shark Week, Pop-Culture Leviathan," *Atlantic*, August 13, 2012, https://www.theatlantic.com/entertainment/archive/2012/08/the -evolution-of-shark-week-pop-culture-leviathan/261063/.

32   Ernest Hemingway, *The Old Man and the Sea* (New York: Charles Scribner's Sons, 1952), 37.

33   Carolyn B. Stegman, *Women of Achievement in Maryland History* (Forestville, MD: Anaconda, 2002), 230, quoted in "Eugenie Clark, Ph.D. (1922–2015)" Archives of Maryland, accessed December 15, 2017, http://msa.maryland.gov/megafile/msa /speccol/sc3500/sc3520/013500/013574/html/13574bio.html.

34   Paul Raffaele, "Forget Jaws, Now It's . . . Brains!," *Smithsonian*, June 2008, http:// www.smithsonianmag.com/science-nature/forget-jaws-now-its-brains-48249580/.

39   Brian Clark Howard, "Through a Shark's Eyes: See How They Glow in the Deep," *National Geographic*, April 25, 2016, http://news.nationalgeographic.com/2016 /04/160425-biofluorescence-glowing-catsharks-shark-eye-camera/.

44   Christopher Crosby, "Can Social Media Give Sharks a Better Reputation?," *Smithsonian*, March 8, 2017, https://www.smithsonianmag.com/innovation/can -social-media-give-sharks-better-reputation-180962411/.

45   Elisabeth von Thorn und Taxis, "Expedition Nantucket: Elisabeth TNT Joins Ocearch to Brave the Great Blue Sea in Hopes of Tagging a Great White Shark," *Vogue*, December 2016, 172.

50   Calla Wahlquist, "Leopard Shark Makes World-First Switch from Sexual to Asexual Reproduction," *Guardian* (London), January 17, 2017.

52   Eric Niler, "Sharks Navigate by Nose," *Seeker*, January 6, 2016, https://www.seeker.com/sharks-navigate-by-nose-1770700197.html.

55   Jim Morrison, "How Speedo Created a Record-Breaking Swimsuit," *Scientific American*, July 27, 2012, https://www.scientificamerican.com/article/how-speedo-created-swimsuit/.

60   Brian Handwerk, "Bull Shark Threat: They Swim Where We Swim," *National Geographic*, July 19, 2005, http://news.nationalgeographic.com/news/2005/07/0719_050719_bullsharks.html.

63   Richard Black, "Sharks Navigate Using 'Mental Maps,'" *BBC*, March 2, 2011, http://www.bbc.com/news/science-environment-12612655.

65   Niler, "Sharks Navigate."

66   Sylvia A. Earle, Twitter post, May 3, 2017, https://twitter.com/SylviaEarle/status/859858107362680838.

69   "Great White Mysteries: Shark Tagging with Ocearch," *CBS This Morning*, January 9, 2012, http://www.tvguide.com/tvshows/cbs-this-morning/video/381939/great-white-mysteries-shark-tagging-with-ocearch-24674418/.

70–71   Greg Marshall, interview with author, March 24, 2011.

72   Phillip S. Lobel, "Diver Eco-Tourism and the Behavior of Reef Sharks and Rays—an Overview," Proceedings of the American Academy of Underwater Sciences 27th Symposium, Dauphin Island, AL, AAUS 2008, accessed December 15, 2017, http://archive.rubicon-foundation.org/xmlui/bitstream/handle/123456789/8012/AAUS_2008_103-13.pdf?sequence=1.

72   Ibid.

73   Greg Skomal, "Seeing Deeper into the White Shark's World," YouTube video, 19:19, posted by TEDx Talks, December 2, 2015, https://www.youtube.com/watch?v=03Ex3obOI1Q.

75   Amy Bounds, "Longmont's Skyline High Students Build Shark Measuring Device for Boulder Researcher," *Longmont (CO) News*, October 6, 2016, http://www.dailycamera.com/longmont-news/ci_30442674/longmonts-skyline-high-students-build-shark-measuring-device.

75   "Staff Spotlight: Dr. Mikki McComb-Kobza," Ocean First Institute, April 7, 2017, https://www.oceanfirstinstitute.org/blog/staff-spotlight-dr-mikki-mccomb-kobza/.

76   Delmarvanow staff, "Tagged off OC, Hell's Bay, the Shark, Sets Travel Record," *USA Today*, January 25, 2017, https://www.usatoday.com/story/news/2017/01/25/tagged-off-oc-hells-bay-shark-sets-travel-record/97030672/.

79   "WHOI Engineers Amy Kukulya and Roger Stokey Discuss REMUS SharkCam," Woods Hole Oceanographic Institution Media Office, accessed November 28, 2017, https://www.whoi.edu/page.do?pid=136616&tid=3622&cid=198909.

80 Clarinda Higgins, former assistant curator of education at the Maritime Aquarium, Norwalk, CT, interview with author via Facebook messaging, June 13, 2017.

83 BEC crew, "Watch: Diver Coaxes Shark into a Tonic State, and It's Beautiful," *Science Alert*, February 11, 2015, http://www.sciencealert.com/watch-diver-coaxes -shark-into-a-tonic-state-and-it-s-beautiful.

88 Laura Gartry, "Ningaloo Whale Shark: 'Big Boys Stumpy and Zorro Make WA [Western Australia] Feeding Trip for 22 Straight Years," *ABC*, October 4, 2016, http://www.abc.net.au/news/2016-10-04/ningaloo-whale-sharks-stumpy-zorro-in -annual-wa-pilgrimage/7902376.

90 Michael Bear, "Issues and Challenges in Marine Science," *OceanSpaces* (blog), August 23, 2016, http://oceanspaces.org/blog/issues-and-challenges-marine-citizen -science.

96 Oliver Milman and Karl Mathiesen, "Monster Shark Tournaments Face Growing Pressure to Reform," *Guardian* (US ed.), July 19, 2016, https://www.theguardian .com/environment/2016/jul/19/atlantic-shark-hunting-tournaments-endangered -species.

96 Svati Kirsten Narula, "Letting Sharks Off the Hook," *Atlantic*, July 26, 2013, https://www.theatlantic.com/national/archive/2013/07/letting-sharks-off-the -hook/278117/.

97 University of British Columbia, "Sharks Worth More in the Ocean Than on the Menu," *Science Daily*, May 30, 2013, https://www.sciencedaily.com /releases/2013/05/130530192429.htm.

99 "Project Leader Alison Kock," Save Our Seas, accessed June 11, 2017. http:// saveourseas.com/project-leader/alison-kock/.

100 "Monwabisi Sikweyiya," Vimeo, accessed December 15, 2017, https://vimeo .com/19214562.

100 Sara-Jayne King, "Shark Spotters SA: Keeping Beaches Safe," LeadSA, January 11, 2017, http://leadsa.co.za/articles/238708/shark-spotters-sa-keeping-beaches-safe.

103 Michael Bear, "Are Sevengill Sharks Making a Comeback?" *Marine Science Today*, June 21, 2011, http://marinesciencetoday.com/2011/06/21/are-sevengill-sharks -making-a-comeback/#ixzz4kqZPRdug.

104 "Fieldscope: Sharks of California," Ocean Sanctuaries Citizen Science Projects, accessed June 23, 2017, http://oceansanctuaries.org/wordpress/citizen-science -projects/fieldscope/.

105 Kate Horowitz, "A New Hammerhead Shark Species May Have Just Been Discovered," *Mental Floss*, February 3, 2017, http://mentalfloss.com/article/91848 /new-hammerhead-shark-species-may-have-just-been-discovered.

GLOSSARY

ACOUSTIC TAGGING: tags that can be attached to animals. They emit sound signals that can be picked up by receivers and allow animals to be detected and tracked.

ADAPTATION: how an animal changes features over generations to better survive in its environment

AMPULLAE OF LORENZINI: sensors in a shark's snout that allow it to pick up electrical signals created by motion in the water

APEX PREDATOR: the top feeder in a food chain

AUTONOMOUS UNDERWATER VEHICLE (AUV): a diving robot operated remotely or by preprogramming without an onboard pilot or a tether linking it to a ship

BARNACLES: crustaceans that anchor onto rocks, shells, boats, or other hard undersea surfaces and that filter seawater to get their food

BENTHIC: seafloor or deep dwelling

BIOFLUORESCENCE: a type of glowing effect created by fluorescent molecules, which absorb and reemit light

BIOLUMINESCENCE: another type of glowing effect created by light-emitting molecules in which an enzyme (luciferase) stimulates a compound called luciferin

BYCATCH: the accidental catch of a fish while fishing for other species

CAUDAL: referring to the tail of a marine animal

CHEMORECEPTION: in sharks, a highly refined sense of smell and taste combined

CHONDRICHTHYES: the class of animals to which all the species of sharks belong

CITIZEN SCIENCE: interested laypeople (not professionals) contributing data they collect from their surroundings and expeditions to scientific researchers

CLASPERS: elongated fins that allow male sharks to hold onto females during mating

CRITTERCAM: a camera that can be attached to an animal to record its behavior and experiences in the wild

DENTICLE: a tooth-shaped scale embedded in sharkskin. The scales make sharks hydrodynamic, assisting them in swimming fast.

DISTRIBUTION: the number of animals over a range of land or sea

DIVERSITY: the number of different species of animals over a range of land or sea

DORSAL: on the back

ECOSYSTEM: a community of living organisms (plants and animals) and nonliving components such as air, water, and soil that interact to create a functioning, interconnected system

ELECTROMAGNETISM: a force created by the interaction between the electrically charged particles in all molecules

ELECTRORECEPTION: the ability to detect electrical charges, such as those created by live animals

ENDOTHERM: the ability of a marine animal to heat its own body to a temperature that is warmer than surrounding water

FOOD CHAIN: a hierarchical system of organisms that rely on one another for nutrition. For example, sharks eat smaller fish that eat smaller krill that eat smaller plankton.

GESTATION PERIOD: the length of time it takes a pregnancy to reach full term (ready for birth)

GILLS: slits on the head and neck of a shark through which water passes, allowing the shark to process the water for oxygen; the breathing organs of a shark

GOPRO: the brand name of a small video camera that can be mounted onto solid surfaces to capture live action, including underwater

HABITAT: the area an organism relies on for nutrition, shelter, mating, and other needs

ICHTHYOLOGIST: a scientist who studies sharks and other fish

ICHTHYOLOGY: the scientific study of sharks and other fish

LATERAL LINE: a row of pressure sensors along a shark's side

MECHANORECEPTION: the ability to detect motion. Shark mechanoreception comes through their lateral lines, ampullae of Lorenzini, and nasal barbels.

NASAL BARBELS: sensors that dangle from a shark's head to allow it to sense prey on or below the seafloor

NICHE: a position in the food chain and environment to which an animal adapts to thrive there

NICTITATING MEMBRANE: an extra eyelid or fold of skin that covers a shark's eye when it attacks another animal. The fold protects the eye from damage.

OSTEICHTHYES: the class of animals to which all the species of bony fish belong

PELAGIC: open ocean

PHOTORECEPTION: a sense of vision and light. In sharks the photoreceptors are extra sensitive to blue light, which allows them to see in deeper, darker waters than humans can.

PLACODERMS: a group of bony fish from which scientists believe sharks evolved

POPULATION: the number of a group of animals of the same species

SPIRACLES: small head organs that assist some species of shark with breathing

STOCKS: the natural number in a population of animals prior to overfishing or other depletions

TELEMETRIC BUOY: an apparatus that sits in or on the surface of water to gather and transmit data. For example, a transmitter tag on a shark sends signals about the shark's location to the buoy, which sends the data by satellite back to a land-based computer where a scientist reads it.

TONIC IMMOBILITY: a state induced by turning a shark upside down, rendering it briefly paralyzed. This state can be useful to some animals that avoid predators by appearing to be dead.

VENTRAL: on the front

SELECTED BIBLIOGRAPHY

Atkins, JoAnn. "Discovered: Possible New Species of Hammerhead Shark." *Florida International University News*, February 2, 2017. http://news.fiu.edu/2017/02 /discovered-possible-new-species-of-hammerhead-shark/108412.

"The Best Shark Facts on Dry Land." Shark Sider. Accessed November 28, 2017. https://www.sharksider.com.

Burgess, George H., and Lindsay French, International Shark Attack File. "ISAF 2016 Worldwide Shark Attack Summary." Florida Museum of Natural History, University of Florida. Accessed December 15, 2017. https://www.floridamuseum.ufl.edu/fish/isaf /worldwide-summary/.

Chow, Denise. "Why Sharks Generate More Money Alive Than Dead." *LiveScience*, May 31, 2013. https://www.livescience.com/37048-shark-economic-value.html.

Fields, A. T., K. A. Feldheim, J. Gelscleichter, C. Pfoertner, and D. D. Chapman. "Population Structure and Cryptic Speciation in Bonnethead Sharks *Sphyrna tiburo* in the South-Eastern U.S.A. and Caribbean." *Journal of Fish Biology*, September 7, 2016. http://onlinelibrary.wiley.com/doi/10.1111/jfb.13025/full.

Gardiner, Jayne M., Nicholas M. Whitney, and Robert M. Hueter. "Smells Like Home: The Role of Olfactory Clues in the Homing Behavior of Blacktip Sharks, *Carcharhinus limbatus*." *Integrative & Comparative Biology*, July 13, 2015. https://academic.oup.com /icb/article/55/3/495/758691.

Guy, Allison. "Maligned as Lazy and Toxic, Greenland Sharks Are Smarter Than You Think." *Oceana*, June 29, 2016. http://oceana.org/blog/maligned-lazy-and-toxic-greenland -sharks-are-smarter-you-think.

Myers, R. A., J. K. Baum, T. D. Shepherd, S. P. Powers, and C. H. Peterson. "Cascading Effects of the Loss of Apex Predatory Sharks from a Coastal Ocean." *Science* 315, no. 5820 (March 30, 2007): 1846–1850. http://www2.ca.uky.edu/Forestry/FOR230 /Cascading%20Effects%20of%20the%20Loss%20of%20Apex%20Predatory%20 Sharks%20Science%202007.pdf.

Nielsen, Julius, Rasmus B. Hedeholm, Jan Heinemeier, Peter G. Bushnell, Jørgen S. Christiansen, Jesper Olsen, Christopher Bronk Ramsey et al. "Eye Lens Radiocarbon Reveals Centuries of Longevity in the Greenland Shark (*Somniosus microcephalus*)." *Science* 353, no. 6300 (August 12, 2016): 702–704. doi:10.1126/science.aaf1703.

Papastamatiou, Yannis P., Daniel P. Cartamil, Christopher G. Lowe, Carl G. Meyer, Brad M. Wetherbee, and Kim N. Holland. "Scales of Orientation, Directed Walks, and Movement Path Structure in Sharks." *Journal of Animal Ecology*, March 1, 2011. http:// besjournals.onlinelibrary.wiley.com/hub/results/?search=papastamatiou&journal-doi =10.1111%2F%28ISSN%291365-2656.

"Shark Guardian 100 Shark Facts." Shark Guardian. Accessed November 28, 2017. https://www.sharkguardian.org/top-100-shark-facts.

Shute, Lauren. "11-Year-Old Sports Fan's Quest to Save Sharks." *Sports Illustrated Kids*, July 3, 2015. https://www.sikids.com/si-kids/2016/01/12/sports-sharks.

Skomal, Gregory, Phillip Lobel, and Greg Marshall. "The Use of Animal-Borne Imaging to Assess Post-Release Behavior as It Relates to Capture Stress in Grey Reef Sharks, *Carcharhinus amblyrhynchos*." *Marine Technology Society Journal* 41, no. 4 (Winter 2007): 44–48. http://www.ingentaconnect.com/content/mts/mtsj/2007/00000041/00000004/art00009.

Taylor & Francis. "The *Jaws* Effect: Biting Review Finds Shark Policy Based on Movie Myths." *ScienceDaily*, December 11, 2014. https://www.sciencedaily.com/releases/2014/12/141211090610.htm.

Vianna, Gabriel M. S., Mark G. Meekan, Tova H. Bornovski, and Jessica J. Meeuwig. "Acoustic Telemetry Validates a Citizen Science Approach for Monitoring Sharks on Coral Reefs." *PLOS One 9*, no 4 (April 2014). doi: 10.1371/journal.pone.0095565.

FURTHER INFORMATION

ACTIVITIES AND CLUBS

Adopt a Shark
> https://gifts.worldwildlife.org/gift-center/gifts/Species-Adoptions.aspx
> The World Wildlife Fund Adopt a Shark program offers you a chance to officially adopt a shark and follow it in its daily life while supporting conservation efforts.

Gills Club
> http://www.gillsclub.org/about
> This club was founded in 2014 by women, with the goal of inspiring and supporting girls interested in sharks and shark research. It's part of the Atlantic White Shark Conservancy, based in Chatham, Massachusetts. Members include girls as well as women shark scientists. Meeting locations include the Cape Cod Museum of Natural History in Massachusetts, the Seattle Aquarium in Washington, and the Mote Marine Laboratory in Sarasota, Florida.

Identify a Shark
> https://www.floridamuseum.ufl.edu/fish/discover/sharks/id-key-sharks/
> The Florida Museum of Natural History/University of Florida offers in-depth information for identifying sharks in the Atlantic Ocean. Check out this site for photographs and a dichotomous key to help you narrow down your shark based on its physical features.

Report Shark Sightings

> http://www.sharkresearchcommittee.com/pacific_coast_shark_news.htm
> For Pacific Coast shark sightings, you can report your sightings to this website by
> providing details about your location and your observation. Read the latest news from
> other contributors at this site.
> http://www.atlanticwhiteshark.org/sharktivity-map/
> For Atlantic Coast shark sightings, report your sightings and track tagged sharks at this
> website. Provide details about your location and your observation and learn about other
> participants' experiences at this spot.

Report Whale Shark Sightings

> http://whaleshark.org
> Wildbook for Whale Sharks allows citizen scientists to contribute photographs and to
> match their sharks with those in the catalog.

Seek Shark Egg Cases

> http://www.sharktrust.org/en/usa_eggcases
> The Save Our Seas Foundation sponsors the Great Eggcase Hunt project. Some people
> call egg cases mermaids' purses. Small egg-laying sharks and rays deposit these egg cases,
> or egg-filled black rectangular pockets, onto rocks, seagrass, and other underwater
> surfaces. The pockets have tentacles at each corner for clinging to surfaces. The Great
> Eggcase Hunt project invites beachcombers, snorkelers, and divers to report empty egg
> cases to help pinpoint shark nurseries.

Shark Stewards Conservation Club

> http://sharkstewards.org/get-involved/
> Learn about starting a school shark club and doing other volunteer work and fund-
> raising for shark conservation and research.

We Love Sharks (Discovery Channel Shark Week)

> http://welovesharks.club
> Find information, news, photographs, and videos, as well as links to shark clothing,
> toys, and other items.

SMARTPHONE APPS

These apps allow you to follow individual sharks on interactive maps. You can see where each
shark is in real time and track where it has been previously.

Global Shark Tracker, Ocearch

> http://www.ocearch.org/tracker/

Sharktivity, Atlantic White Shark Conservancy

> http://www.atlanticwhiteshark.org/sharktivity-map/

Track Tagged Sharks
You can follow tagged sharks in a variety of different ways and through technologies provided by various institutions. Below are two examples:
Use Twitter to follow daily postings from citizen scientists and researchers about the whereabouts and activities of popular sharks.
Track a tiger shark tagged by the Guy Harvey Research Institute at http://cnso.nova.edu/ghri/tiger-sharks/.

WEBSITES

Atlantic White Shark Conservancy
http://www.atlanticwhiteshark.org
Enter contests (for example, to win a ticket for a great white shark expedition in Cape Cod) and learn about and support the research of shark scientists in the North Atlantic Ocean.

The Shark Lab, California State University, Long Beach
http://www.csulb.edu/natural-sciences-mathematics-biological-sciences/explore/shark-lab
Follow the work of Chris Lowe's SharkLab, and learn about Shark Week.

Shark Zone, Center for Shark Research, Marine Mote Laboratory
https://mote.org/exhibits/details/shark-zone
Learn the history of shark research, get information about the aquarium here, find out about internships, and more.

BOOKS

Benchley, Peter, and Karen Wojtyla. *Shark Life: True Stories about Sharks and the Sea*. New York: Yearling, 2007. Adapted from Peter Benchley. *Shark! True Stories and Lessons from the Deep*. New York: Collins, 2002.

Clark, Eugenie. *The Lady and the Sharks*. Sarasota, FL: Peppertree, 2010.

Cousteau, Jacques-Yves. *The Shark: Splendid Savage of the Sea*. Garden City, NY: Doubleday, 1970.

Downer, Ann. *The Animal Mating Game*. Minneapolis: Twenty-First Century Books, 2017.

Montgomery, Sy. *The Great White Shark Scientist*. Boston: Houghton Mifflin, 2017.

Muller, Michael. *Sharks: Face-to-Face with the Ocean's Endangered Predator*. New York: Taschen, 2016.

Musick, John A., and Beverly McMillan. *The Shark Chronicles: A Scientist Tracks the Consummate Predator*. New York: Henry Holt, 2002.

Young, Karen Romano. *Whale Quest*. Minneapolis: Twenty-First Century Books, 2018.

Zimmer, Marc. *Bioluminescence: Nature and Science at Work*. Minneapolis: Twenty-First Century Books, 2016.

VIDEOS

"Great White Mysteries: Shark Tagging with Ocearch." *CBS This Morning*, January 9, 2012. http://www.tvguide.com/tvshows/cbs-this-morning/video/381939/great-white-mysteries-shark-tagging-with-ocearch-24674418/.
Watch this interview with Chris Fischer about the work of tagging sharks aboard *Ocearch*.

"October 21, 2017, Off Chatham, Cape Cod." Atlantic Great White Shark Conservancy. https://www.boston.com/news/local-news/2017/10/23/this-graphic-video-captured-a-great-white-shark-devouring-a-seal-off-cape-cod.
In this video filmed at the beach, a great white shark attacks a seal.

"REMUS SharkCam: The Hunter and the Hunted." WHOI Oceanographic Systems Lab, 2013. http://www.whoi.edu/remus-sharkcam/hunterandhunted.
This video taken by AUV glider REMUS shows sharks in their natural habitat—and how they react to the glider.

"Seeing Deeper into the White Shark's World—Greg Skomal—TedxNewBedford." YouTube video, 19:19. Posted by TEDxTalks, December 2, 2015. https://www.youtube.com/watch?v=03Ex3obOI1Q.
Shark researcher Greg Skomal describes his path to becoming a scientist and studying sharks.

INDEX

ancient shark species, 20–21, 38, 42
  Carcharodon megalodon, 21
  ichthyosaur, 38
  Squalicorax, 20
apex predator, 8, 44–46
aquariums, 49, 50, 83–86, 91, 98, 103
  Birch Aquarium, 63
  Georgia Aquarium, 84–86
  Maritime Aquarium, 81
  Monterey Bay Aquarium, 84
  New York Aquarium, 82
  Okinawa Churaumi Aquarium, 82
  Reef HQ Aquarium, 50
  SeaWorld, 83
  Virginia Aquarium & Marine Science Center, 49
autonomous underwater vehicles (AUVs), 76, 78

benthic (seafloor) sharks, 22, 25
bioluminescence, 113
bycatch, 14, 44, 85, 94
  drift gill nets, 15
  longliners, 14

citizen science, 93, 103–105
Clark, Eugenie, 11–13, 30, 33, 68, 82, 91
coastal sharks, 22, 59
commercial use of sharks
  cartilage, 16
  fins, 15, 16–17
  meat, 16–17, 38
  medicine, 17
  oil, 16
  skin, 16–17
conservation
  Convention on International Trade in
    Endangered Species of Wild Fauna and Flora
    (CITES), 10, 15
  International Union for Conservation of
    Nature (IUCN), 96, 101, 105, 106
  IUCN Shark Specialist Group (IUCN SSC), 96
  Ningaloo Marine Park, 88
  Ocean Sanctuaries (and Citizen Science
    Project), 104
  Save Our Seas Foundation, 99
  US Shark Conservation Act of 2010, 17
Cousteau, Jacques, 12–13, 91

Discovery Channel, 13, 91
  Shark Week, 13, 91, 98
distribution of sharks, 14, 101

ecotourism, 96–98
endangered sharks, 49, 101, 106

feeding and eating patterns, 8, 15, 19, 22, 24, 25, 28,
  32–34, 40–43, 44, 50, 54, 59, 61–62, 82–84
finning, 17

Gills Club, 98

hadrosaurus, 20

ichthyologists
  Alison Kock, 8, 34, 66, 71, 99
  Andrew Nosal, 63–64
  Eugenie Clark, 11–13, 30, 33, 68, 82, 91
  Gregory Skomal, 69–71, 73, 75–76, 78, 91
  Mahmood Shivji, 67, 76, 89
  Mikki McComb-Kobza, 75
  Phillip Lobel, 71–72, 78
iNaturalist, 105
infographics, 24, 30, 56–57, 59, 61, 92, 100

mesopredators, 45–46
mutualism, 48

National Marine Fisheries Service (NMFS), 93–94
National Oceanographic and Atmospheric
  Administration (NOAA), 95, 96

pelagic (open ocean) sharks, 19, 22–23, 25, 59,
  82, 96
population of sharks, 14, 16–17, 44–46, 69–70,
  93, 96
predation, 7, 8, 16, 28, 38, 42, 44–46, 53–54
prey, 8–9, 25, 28, 29, 34, 35, 37, 39, 40, 42–43,
  44–45, 53–54, 58–59, 84

research organizations
  Bimini Biological Field Station Sharklab, 98
  Dalhousie University, 10, 14–15
  Ecocean, 86–88, 104
  Guy Harvey Research Institute (GHRI), 67, 76
  Hawai'i Institute of Marine Biology, 72
  Mote Marine Laboratory, 45
  Ocean First Institute, 75
  Pacific Shark Research Center, 98
  Reef Environmental Education Foundation
    (REEF), 102
  Save Our Seas Foundation (SOSF) Shark
    Research Center, 99
  Scripps Institution of Oceanography, 63
  Sevengill Shark Identification Project, 103

Shark Lab at California State University, Long Beach, 77
University of Florida, 9
Woods Hole Oceanographic Institution, 78

safety tips, 100, 103–104
Sharctic Circle, 38
shark adaptation and evolution
  camouflage, 28
  endothermy, 28
  heat regulation, 28, 38
  hydrodynamics, 26, 38, 53, 55
  ram ventilation, 29
  sinusoidal movement, 53–54
  tonic immobility, 83
shark anatomy, 24, 107–114
  eyes, 27, 28, 34–35, 38
  fins, 15–17, 21, 25, 27–28, 40, 47, 53
  gills, 15, 21, 25, 27, 28–30, 42, 84
  jaws, 21–22, 26, 40, 42
  tail, 18, 24–25, 38, 40, 52–54, 88
  teeth, 20, 22, 27, 30, 40–43, 47
shark attacks
  International Shark Attack File (ISAF), 9–10
  teeth, 5–11, 13, 28, 35, 40, 42, 78–79, 84
shark behavior
  hunting, 8–9, 22, 25, 34, 40, 43, 48, 54, 70–71, 111
  mating and reproduction, 17, 26, 32, 39, 46–47, 49–50, 59, 61, 73, 82, 86–88
  migration, 8, 12, 22, 41, 52, 58–59, 61–62, 67, 76–77, 94
  navigation, 37, 62–65
  speed, 22, 25, 28, 33, 38, 40, 42, 53–54, 67, 71, 78
shark diet, 20, 87, 107–114
shark fin soup, 16–17
shark genome, 87–88
shark habitat
  benthic, 22, 25
  coastal, 22, 47, 51, 58–60, 64
  pelagic, 19, 22–23, 25, 59, 82, 96
  shallow water, 22, 36, 47, 50, 60, 77, 103, 113
shark identification, 27, 28, 42, 86, 95, 104, 106
shark life cycle, 82
shark migration, 8, 12, 22, 41, 52, 58–59, 61–62, 67, 76–77, 94
shark reproduction
  nurseries, 50–51
  parthenogenesis, 49–50
  pregnancy, 17, 49, 73, 113

shark respiration, 28
shark senses
  ampullae of Lorenzini, 36–37, 63
  chemoreception, 35–36, 38
  electroreception, 36–37
  mechanoreception, 36
  photoreception, 34–35
sharks in art, 5–6
sharks in books/print
  Lady with a Spear (Clark), 11
  The Old Man and the Sea (Hemingway), 32
  Shark Life (Benchley and Wojtyla), 8
  Sharks of New England (De Maddalena and Heim), 4
sharks in captivity, 81–82, 84–86
sharks in film
  The Deep, 7
  Jaws, 4–5, 7–8, 33, 90
sharks in mythology
  aumakua, 13
  kahuna, 13
sharkskin
  dermal denticles, 26
  placoid scales, 26
  shagreen, 58
sharks on television
  The Beast (1996 miniseries), 7
  The Undersea World of Jacques Cousteau, 12
Shark Stewards, 105
spyhopping, 39
squalene, 23
Summer of the Shark, 6
swimming, 4–5, 7, 9–11, 14, 19, 21–23, 25, 29–30, 34, 38, 40–41, 46, 48, 52–55, 58–63, 67, 69–70, 72–73, 76, 78, 81, 82–85, 87, 90, 99–100, 103
symbiosis, 48

tagging sharks
  acoustic tags, 68–69, 73–74, 77, 91, 99, 102
  Cooperative Shark Tagging Program, 93–95
  Pop-Off Satellite Archival Tags (PSATs), 74
  Rototags, 93, 95
  satellite tags, 22, 51, 68, 74–77
  Smart Position or Temperature Transmitting (SPOT) tags, 74
  tagging guide, 74
  Watermen Project, 98
technology
  cameras, 12–13, 31, 39, 70–71, 74–75, 77–79, 91–93, 99

drones, 77–78, 93
Speedo Fastskin FSII, 55
Speedo LZR suit, 55
telemetry buoys, 101
threats to sharks
bacteria, 15
commercial and recreational fishing, 10,
14–17, 19, 44–45, 93
infection, 15
noise, 15
water pollution, 15, 17
tracking sharks
autonomous underwater vehicles (AUVs),
75–76, 78
Exploration Vessel (E/V) Nautilus, 31
Hercules (ROV)—EVN submersible, 31

Ocearch's Global Shark Tracker, 68
REMUS (Remote Environmental Monitoring
Units), 78–79
Sevengill Shark Tracker, 104
SharkCam, 78–79
SharksCount Program, 90
Shark Spotters Programme, 99–100

Wildbook database, 86–88, 104

PHOTO ACKNOWLEDGMENTS

The images in this book are used with the permission of: Backgrounds, Marble background/ Shutterstock.com; doodles provided by author: 56–57 (https://tinyurl.com/y9xpxj7r), 92 (https://tinyurl.com/ya9sf8hx); Movie Poster Image Art/agency/Getty Images, p. 5; Photo 12/ UIG/Getty Images, p. 6; © Dan Burton/naturepl.com, p. 10; Independent Picture Service, p. 11; Keystone-France/Gamma-Keystone/Getty Images, p. 12; Andre Seale/Alamy Stock Photo, p. 14; Sijori Images/Barcroft Images/Getty Images, p. 16; Kelvin Aitken/VWPics/ Alamy Stock Photo, p. 19; Colin Keates/Dorling Kindersley/Getty Images, p. 20; John Cancalosi/Photolibrary/Getty Images, p. 21; PLACEHOLDER FOR 23; Laura Westlund/ Independent Picture Service, pp. 24, 30, 59, 61, 97, 107–114; © SeaPics.com, pp. 26, 38; Martin Prochazkacz/Shutterstock.com, p. 27; atese/iStock/Getty Images Plus/Getty Images, p. 29; USO/iStock/Getty Images Plus/Getty Images, p. 33; © Richard Robinson/naturepl. com, p. 35; © Alex Mustard/naturepl.com, p. 36; Borut Furlan/WaterFrame/Getty Images, p. 37; © Bruce Rasner/Rotman/naturepl.com, p. 42; Charles Hood/Alamy Stock Photo, p. 43; Ger Bosma/Alamy Stock Photo, p. 46; © Doug Perrine/naturepl.com, pp. 47, 51; © David Doubilet/National Geographic Stock, p. 49; © Nuno Sa/naturepl.com, p. 53; Borut Furlan/ WaterFrame/Getty Images, p. 60; Fiona Ayerst/Shutterstock.com, p. 62; Tobias Bernhard/ Oxford Scientific/Getty Images, p. 64; Guido Floren/Alamy Stock Photo, p. 73; Supplied by WENN.com/Newscom, p. 79; Bill Kennedy/Alamy Stock Photo, p. 80; Reinhard Dirscherl/ WaterFrame/Getty Images, p. 85; imageBROKER/Alamy Stock Photo, p. 91; Courtesy of the National Oceanic and Atmospheric Administration Central Library Photo Collection, p. 94; Jessica Rinaldi/Globe Staff/Getty Images, p. 98; Courtesy the City of Cape Town, p. 100; Maica/iStock/Getty Images Plus/Getty Images, p. 102.

Front cover: Brad Leue/Alamy Stock Photo.

ABOUT THE AUTHOR

Karen Romano Young has dived to the bottom of the Pacific Ocean in a tiny submarine, crunched through Arctic ice in an icebreaker, and visited labs, museum workshops, and research institutions across the United States to write and draw about science. She was a lead science communications fellow aboard Dr. Robert Ballard's research ship *Exploration Vessel Nautilus*.

Young is also an award-winning author who has written and/or illustrated more than thirty books for young readers, and she is the creator of AntarcticLog (#AntarcticLog), a weekly comic about science exploration and the climate. Her nonfiction books include *Whale Quest, Space Junk, Try This!* and *Try This Extreme!* Her fiction work includes *The Beetle and Me: A Love Story*, the graphic novel *Doodlebug: A Novel in Doodles*, and *Hundred Percent*. Her next novel is *The Librarian's Child*, due out in 2019.

She lives with her family in the woods of Bethel, Connecticut. Her next adventure is a stint at Palmer Station, Antarctica, as the recipient of the National Science Foundation's Antarctic Artists and Writers Grant. She has not yet traveled to space.